Lesson Plans Using Graphic Organizers, Grade 6

Table of Contents

Introduction

What is a good education? There are many different answers to that question and differences of opinion regarding what a good education is. One way that states decided to clarify this question was by developing educational standards. These standards detail what students should know and be able to do in each subject area at a given grade level. Standards are high and consistent expectations for all students.

Teachers use classroom activities and assessments to determine if students are meeting or exceeding established standards. With a heavy emphasis being placed on these assessments and the adoption of these standards, the focus of education becomes not just what teachers teach but also what students learn. Teachers must focus their classroom efforts on students' meeting and exceeding standards.

Because there is such strong emphasis placed on these standards and assessments, teachers are in need of lessons and graphic organizers that they can use to ensure that they are covering the standards. The purpose of this book is to provide detailed lessons in correlation to the standards listed in Steck-Vaughn's *Parents' Guide to Standards* (ISBN 0-8172-6184-2) using Madeline Hunter's model of anticipatory set, purpose, input, modeling, guided practice, checking for understanding, independent practice, and closure. These steps provide an effective model for enhancing and maximizing learning:

- Anticipatory Set: a short activity to focus the students' attention before the actual lesson begins
- Purpose: the reason the students need to learn this skill
- Input: the things the students need to be familiar with in order to understand the skill successfully (i.e., vocabulary words, concepts, etc.)
- Modeling: what the teacher shows in graphic form or what the finished product will look like
- Guided Practice: the teacher leading students through the necessary steps to perform the skill
- Checking for Understanding: the teacher asking questions to determine if the students understand the skill and can apply it independently
- Independent Practice: the students working independently to apply the new skill
- Closure: the wrapup of the lesson.

Each lesson consists of a lesson plan, a model, and reproducible practice and individual activities. Each lesson also contains a graphic organizer as a teaching and learning tool for each skill. These tools can be applied to other activities and are interchangeable across the curriculum. These lessons provide a resource to begin implementing the standards and ensuring students' mastery of these skills.

Organization

Each of the four units contains a variety of lessons and activities that correlate to specific standards for sixth grade in the areas of reading, math, science, and social studies.

- **Reading:** The lessons in the reading section are designed to address most of the standards for Language Arts. The activities provide graphic organizers and lessons that allow students to read and understand a variety of materials, to respond to literature in various ways, to use literary terminology, and to use comprehension strategies such as comparing and contrasting, finding main idea, understanding fact and opinion, and summarizing. These lessons and activities can be modified to reach multiple intelligences.

- **Math:** The lessons in the math section are designed to address several of the math standards for sixth grade. They provide the opportunity for the students to construct, read, and interpret data including tables, charts, and graphs. They will also explore various ways to find area and volume, to understand relationships in problem solving situations, and to practice reasoning used in solving these problems.

- **Science:** In addressing the standards, these lessons allow the students to understand the purpose of scientific investigations, ask questions, state predictions, make observations, give reasonable explanations for data collected, use the data to make tables and charts, and organize observations in written form.

- **Social Studies:** The lessons in this section are designed to address several standards for sixth-grade social studies. They encourage students to observe the relationships between regions of the United States, to explore early civilizations, and to strengthen map skills.

Standards

This is a list of the standards adapted into the lesson plans and activities used, although not all of them are represented in this book.

Reading:
- Examine word structure and apply that to developing vocabulary
- Identify story elements in a narrative poem, including characters, setting, and plot
- Apply thinking skills to reading, writing, speaking, listening, and viewing
- Identify fact and opinion in a given passage
- Summarize information from a story
- Identify the cause and the effect
- Identify the main idea and important details of a passage

Math:
- Find the area and circumference of a circle, and apply skills to word problems
- Make predictions and compare results using experimental probability of one variable
- Plot information on a grid, and identify points on a graph
- Demonstrate the concept of volume of squares and rectangles
- Estimate and solve for the mean, mode, and median
- Identify the relationships among the concepts of fractions and decimals
- Use relative frequency to find probability

Science:
- Organize and analyze data from experiments and investigations, and relate studies to natural systems
- Design and conduct experiments using simple machines
- Measure energy
- Identify ecosystems and their attributes
- Identify the characteristics of healthy, functioning ecosystems
- Identify the recessive and dominant genes in living organisms
- Observe the different life cycles in different ecosystems

Social Studies:
- Use contour and aerial photography maps
- Identify and locate physical and human features in the United States as they relate to each unit
- Identify the distinguishing characteristics of the major regions in the Colonial period
- Research historical cultures that had an impact on North America
- Examine the relationship between regions and immigration

Dear Parent,

To ensure that your child has a successful year and meets the requirements to advance to the next grade, our district has developed standards that each child must master. I focus my lessons on those skills listed in each standard to make sure your child receives the proper instruction for those skills. During this school year, our class will be working with activities in reading, mathematics, science, and social studies. We will be completing activities that provide practice to ensure mastery of these important skills. You can play an active role in your child's education. There are many things that you can do to help your child gain a good education.

From time to time, I may send home activity sheets. To help your child, please consider the following suggestions.

- Provide a quiet place for your child to study or do homework. Make sure your child has all the supplies necessary to complete the work.
- Set a time for your child to study or do homework. This will help your child manage time better.
- Go over the activity's directions together. Make sure your child knows what he or she is supposed to do.
- Give help when needed, but remember that the activity is your child's responsibility.
- Check the activity when it is done. Go over any parts your child may have had trouble completing.
- Help your child study for tests by asking sample questions or going over the material to be covered.
- Review all of the work your child brings home, and note improvements as well as activities that need reviewing.

Together we can help your child maintain a positive attitude about the activities while ensuring academic growth and success. Let your child know that each activity provides an opportunity to have fun and to learn. Above all, enjoy this time you spend with your child. He or she will feel your support, and skills will improve with each activity's completion!

Thank you for your help!

Cordially,

List of Graphic Organizers

(Tool 1) Identifying Characters' Feelings

Preparation: Make copies of pages 9 and 10. Make an overhead of pages 8 and 9.

Anticipatory Set: Ask the students if they have ever watched a television show that made them feel the show was about their lives. Ask them why they felt that way and to give examples.

Purpose: Explain that sometimes people relate to characters in movies, television shows, and books because they relate to the characters' feelings. The students are going to identify characters' feelings in several passages.

Input: Explain that by understanding the characters' feelings, the students will get more meaning from the story.

Modeling: Place page 8 on the overhead. With the students, read over the directions and sample passage. Discuss with them the feelings of the characters. Ask the students to explain how they know the characters' feelings. Then go over the questions for each passage. Have the students support their answers with examples from the passage.

Guided Practice: Explain that the students are going to read another passage and identify the main character's feelings. They will read the passage with a partner and highlight at least six examples of the character's feelings in the passage. Then they will discuss the feelings with their partners, and they will support their answers with information from the story.

Check for Understanding: As a whole group, discuss some of the feelings that the main character had. Have several students provide an example and support for their answers.

Independent Practice: Now that they are aware of several of the main character's feelings, the students will complete the graphic organizer. They will list the main character in the center square, and in the circles surrounding the square, they will give examples of his or her feelings and the reason for those feelings. The students will work independently.

Closure: Review why it is important to understand characters' feelings in literature. Have the students give examples from other stories they have read that reveal how the characters feel. Then discuss how the stories would be if they did not express any of the characters' feelings.

Characters' Feelings

Directions

Read the steps below.

Remember, To Understand the Feelings of Characters:
1. READ the story carefully.
2. LOOK for clues about how the characters are feeling.
3. THINK about those feelings to gain an understanding of the characters.

Read each selection. Darken the answer circle by the choice that best answers the question.

Lacey came in from school and threw down her books. Homework could wait. She ran into the backyard and called for her new puppy. When Lacey knelt down to hug him, he gave her sloppy kisses in return.

1. How does Lacey feel?
Ⓐ scared
Ⓑ disappointed
Ⓒ angry
Ⓓ excited

2. Why does Lacey feel that way?
Ⓐ Her puppy seems to be sick.
Ⓑ Lacey has to do homework.
Ⓒ Lacey has a new puppy.
Ⓓ School is out for the year.

Sean walked slowly back from the mailbox. "I can't believe it," he said. "They said my model would be here in two to four weeks, and it's been five weeks now."

3. How does Sean feel?
Ⓐ disappointed
Ⓑ cheerful
Ⓒ frightened
Ⓓ excited

4. Why does he feel that way?
Ⓐ He couldn't mail his letter today.
Ⓑ His model had arrived broken.
Ⓒ Sean has lost his mom's mail.
Ⓓ He is tired of waiting.

It's How You Look at It

Everybody knew that Jake's father collected junk. Well, it looked like junk, anyway. When you drove by their house, you could see all that old stuff out back in the weeds, and their garage was one huge junk warehouse. Jake was quiet at school, and he didn't bring friends home. No one had any real complaints about Jake, but no one knew him well, either, so he never quite seemed to fit in. The other students didn't go out of their way to get better acquainted with Jake. He must be strange—what kind of people would collect all that junk?

One day Jake's class was assigned a task in science. They were put into groups and told to create a space vehicle out of scraps, trash, and other found objects. They were instructed not to spend any money on their project. Grading was to be done on imagination and ingenuity.

While most of the class was wondering where on Earth they would find these objects, Jake's mind immediately set to cataloguing what his father had stored in his garage and in the backyard. He could picture some great possibilities. He figured he probably had enough stuff to make ten space vehicles! He knew his dad wouldn't mind, either. He would say what he always said, "Hey, that's what the stuff is for. Help yourself!"

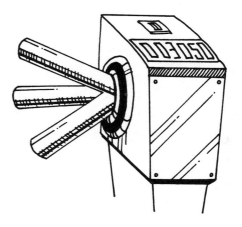

As the days went by, the rest of the groups began to hear about what was happening in Jake's group. While the rest of the class expressed their admiration for the plans Jake's group had drawn up, Jake suddenly realized that he had taken all his resources for granted. These other kids didn't have half the stuff his group had at its disposal. He shyly offered the whole class an opportunity to come to his house and take whatever they wanted. Everyone was appreciative of Jake and his father's generosity. Suddenly, Jake's yard and garage seemed to be filled with treasure instead of junk, and the whole class built such interesting vehicles that they were prominently displayed for the rest of the year.

Name _____ Date _____

Feelings Chart

Directions
Read the passage. Write the main character's name in the center square. In the surrounding circles, write examples of the main character's feelings and support it with details from the passage.

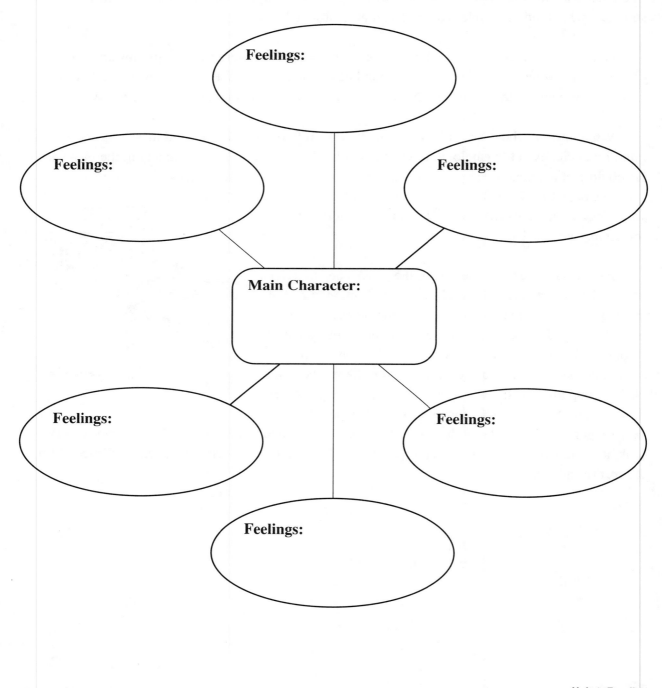

10

(Tool 2) Identifying Fact and Opinion

Preparation: Make copies of pages 13 and 14. Make an overhead of page 12.

Anticipatory Set: Ask your students to tell you the difference between these two statements: *There are four oceans in the world*, and *The water is too cold to swim in the ocean*. Have them try to define *fact* and *opinion* based on those two statements.

Purpose: Explain to the students that they will be looking for examples of facts and opinions from several passages.

Input: Define *fact* as something that is true information, whereas an *opinion* is a belief based on personal ideas.

Modeling: Place page 12 on the overhead. Read the directions for finding facts and opinions. Then read the first passage out loud to the students. Choose an example from the story that is a fact. Then, ask a student to identify one opinion from the passage. Repeat this for the next passage about Venus.

Guided Practice: Now, divide the students into partners. They will read the two passages on page 13 and identify at least one fact and one opinion from each passage. They will write their examples in the boxes.

Check for Understanding: After the students have completed their partner work, review the definitions of *fact* and *opinion*. Read the first passage on page 13 out loud to the whole group. Ask for several volunteers to state their examples of facts and opinions. Discuss the answers to verify they are truly facts and opinions.

Independent Practice: Review the definitions of *fact* and *opinion*. Then pass out the independent practice work on page 14. The students will read the passages and identify one example of fact and one of opinion for each passage.

Closure: Ask the students to think about why it is important to recognize facts and opinions in a work of literature. Discuss with them how opinions can affect the story. Ask them to think of real world examples of how opinions can be detrimental to others.

That's What You Think!

Directions

Read the steps below.

> **To Distinguish Between Fact and Opinion:**
> 1. READ the statement carefully.
> 2. THINK about its meaning.
> 3. DECIDE whether it is a fact or an opinion.

Now, read each story. Identify one fact and one opinion from the story.

1.   Poison ivy is a common, poisonous plant. It has three leaflets on each stem and white berries. Poison ivy can grow as a bush or as a vine. Its leaves are green and shiny in the summer. In the fall, they are a beautiful shade of red. Some people can have a severe reaction if they come into contact with any part of the plant. The poisonous juice is present in the leaves, stem, and flowers. Many people think that any plant with three leaves and white berries should be avoided to prevent possible poisoning.

   Fact: **Opinion:**

2.   The planet Venus was named for the goddess of beauty. It is a lovely name. Venus is the brightest object in the sky except for the Sun and Moon. It is the "morning star" or "evening star" that is often seen. Venus is never seen in the middle of the night. Some people think of it as a mysterious planet because its surface is always covered with clouds. Venus is about the size of Earth and is the closest of all the known planets to Earth.

   Fact: **Opinion:**

Name _____   Date _____

What Do You Think?

Directions

Read each story. Identify one fact and one opinion from the story.

1.   Captain Kidd was a horrible pirate who was eventually hanged for his crimes. He was once an ordinary seaman. The king of England sent him to capture pirates in the Red Sea and the Indian Ocean. No one heard from him for a while. Many people believed he was dead. Then, stories were heard that Captain Kidd had become a pirate himself. When he sailed into New York harbor, he was captured. He defended himself by saying the pirates made him become one of them.

   Fact: **Opinion:**

2.   People learned to raise pigs long ago. Pigs are also called hogs, or swine. They are raised for their meat, fat, and skin. Many people think that pigs are very dirty, but they roll in the mud to cool their bodies and to avoid insects. Pigs are thought by many people to be very bright animals. They can be trained as pets, but it isn't done very often.

   Fact: **Opinion:**

Name _____   Date _____

In My Opinion...

Directions

Read each story. Identify one fact and one opinion in each story.

1.   Many geologists, or earth scientists, believe the seven continents were once one large continent. This idea is not a new one. A German scientist suggested this idea about sixty years ago, but the idea was laughed at by other scientists. When people look at the shape of the continents, they often think they might fit together. This is one part of the argument for a supercontinent. Another piece of evidence is matching fossils that have been found in Africa and South America. Also, tropical plant fossils have been found in Antarctica. The idea of floating continents is a very interesting one.

      Fact: **Opinion:**

2.   Moose are the largest of all antlered animals. The Alaskan moose is the largest moose of all, some of them weighing as much as 1,800 pounds. Some Alaskan bull moose have been measured at $7\frac{1}{2}$ feet at the shoulder. Their antlers reach to 10 feet above the ground. These antlers can weigh 95 pounds and reach widths of 6 feet and more. The size of these animals is amazing.

      Fact: **Opinion:**

Tool 3 Identifying Cause and Effect

Preparation: Copy pages 17 and 18 for students. Make page 16 an overhead.

Anticipatory Set: Turn off the lights in your room. Ask what happened. Then, ask the students why it happened. Explain that the lights went off because you flipped the switch. The switch was the cause for the lights going out.

Purpose: Explain that things happen for a reason. There are causes and effects. Define *cause* and *effect*, and explain that the students are going to identify cause and effect in a passage.

Input: Define *cause* as the reason something happens and *effect* as what happens.

Modeling: Put page 16 on the overhead. Read the directions out loud. Then review the definitions of *cause* and *effect*. Have one student read the first passage. Then ask for a volunteer to use the passage to find the cause for problem number 1. Then ask for a volunteer to find the effect for number 2. Read the second passage out loud, and ask a student to use the passage to find the cause.

Guided Practice: Divide the class into partners. Pass out page 17. Have the students read the passages and use the passages to find the missing causes or effects with their partners.

Check for Understanding: Refocus, and ask a student to define *cause* and *effect*. Then, read the passages on page 17 out loud, and ask for volunteers to give you the effects or causes from the passages.

Independent Practice: Pass out the independent practice on page 18. Explain that the students will read the passages and write in the missing causes or effects.

Closure: Review the definitions of *cause* and *effect*. Ask a student to provide a real world example of a cause and an effect. Then, have a student state an effect, and have another student suggest the cause. Ask for students to think about other subjects and situations that require the use of cause and effect.

Name _____ Date _____

The What and the Why

Directions

Read the steps below.

To Understand Cause and Effect:
1. READ the sentence carefully.
2. LOOK for the clue words.
3. DECIDE which part of the sentence is the cause and which part is the effect.

Now, read each story. Write in the missing cause or effect.

Over 2,000 years ago, Plato said there had been another continent called Atlantis. He said it had sunk because of an earthquake. Scientists haven't found any evidence that Plato's idea is true, so it is considered by most people to be untrue. Some people, however, continue to believe in Atlantis.

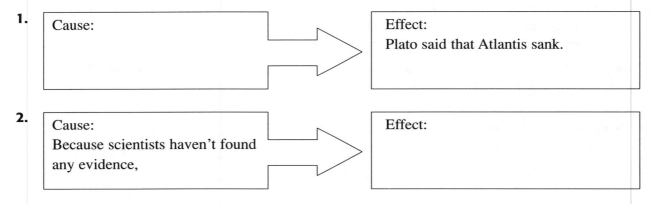

1.
| Cause: | Effect: Plato said that Atlantis sank. |

2.
| Cause: Because scientists haven't found any evidence, | Effect: |

Ms. Rogers built a fence around her backyard so her dog could exercise safely. Because the fencing would be very expensive, she thought carefully before spending her money. After the five-foot fence was completed, the dog was allowed to run freely in the yard. Unfortunately, the fence is now useless because the dog has learned to jump over it.

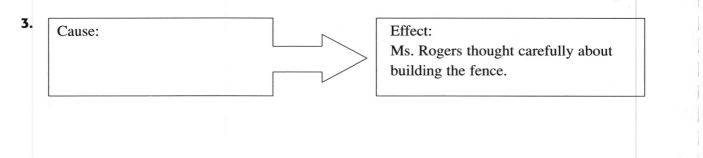

3.
| Cause: | Effect: Ms. Rogers thought carefully about building the fence. |

Name _____ Date _____

The Cause and the Effect

Directions

Read each story. Write in the missing cause or effect.

Coffee is a popular drink in the United States. It is made from the seeds of the coffee plant. These seeds are called coffee "beans" because they look like beans to us. Coffee is grown in a warm climate because it cannot stand any frost at all. Most coffee plantations are in South or Central America. Coffee contains the drug caffeine, which is a stimulant. It is called a stimulant because it increases body activity. Many people drink coffee to wake themselves up in the morning.

1.
| Cause: Because coffee cannot stand any frost, | → | Effect: |

2.
| Cause: | → | Effect: the seeds of the coffee plant are called coffee "beans." |

Bonita's mother was worried about her because her school work was not as good as it had been. Bonita seemed to try hard, but she was making mistakes in work done at school. Her teacher suggested that Bonita have her eyes examined because sometimes poor eyesight can cause this kind of problem. Bonita was nervous because she had never been to an eye doctor. After the tests, the doctor told Bonita that she needed glasses. Bonita is now amazed at the things she can see because of the glasses.

3.
| Cause: Because she had never been to an eye doctor, | → | Effect: |

Name _____ Date _____

The Reason Why

Directions

Read each story. Write in the missing cause or effect.

The Pueblo Indians of today have as their ancestors the cliff dwellers. They were called cliff dwellers because their homes were built on the side of cliffs. These homes were built over 200 years before Christopher Columbus landed in America. The cliff dwellers were farmers who raised corn and beans. The cliff dwellings were easy to defend against enemies because they were so hard to reach. About 700 years ago, the cliff dwellers left their homes. Some historians believe they left because of a drought, a long period with no rain. No one really knows why these remarkable homes were abandoned.

1.

| Cause: Because the cliff dwellings were so hard to reach, | → | Effect: |

2.

| Cause: | → | Effect: some historians believe the cliff dwellers left. |

Blanca had practiced all spring because she wanted to do a good job on the softball team this summer. Her brother had pitched to her so she could practice batting. She had played catch to improve the way she handled the ball. Her coach, Mrs. Wilson, noticed the big improvement. Because Blanca played so well, she was selected as the Most Valuable Player at the end of the season.

3.

| Cause: Because she wanted to improve her batting, | → | Effect: |

Tool 4 Finding the Main Idea

Preparation: Make copies of pages 21 and 22. Make an overhead of page 20.

Anticipatory Set: Ask the students to tell what their favorite movie is. Have them describe it in one sentence. Explain that they are telling you what the story is mostly about.

Purpose: Explain that they are going to find the main idea of several passages.

Input: Define *main idea* as what the story is mostly about. *Details* are the information that supports the main idea.

Modeling: Place page 20 on the overhead. Read the first passage out loud, and ask the students if they can tell you what it is mostly about. Write the response in the middle of the graphic organizer. Then ask them what details support that main idea. Write the details in the surrounding boxes. Do the second example together.

Guided Practice: Divide the students into groups. Pass out the practice sheet, page 21. Have the students read the two paragraphs and use the graphic organizers to find the main idea and details of each paragraph. Monitor the students as they work.

Check for Understanding: Refocus the group, and have one student define *main idea*. Ask one student to volunteer to tell the main idea of the first paragraph on page 21. Then have the students explain the details. Repeat for the second paragraph.

Independent Practice: Pass out page 22. Have the students read the paragraphs and complete the graphic organizers independently.

Closure: Review what *main idea* and *details* are. Ask the students how finding the main idea can be applied to real world situations.

Name _____ Date _____

Getting the Main Idea

Directions

Read each passage. Then fill in the main idea and supporting details.

1.   Peter had worked with his dad fixing things around the house even before he had started school. He knew how to take almost anything apart and put it back together correctly. He had fixed his Aunt Jennifer's car when it was making a horrible grinding sound. When his sister's stereo speaker wasn't making any sound, Peter tinkered with it for an hour and soon had it working better than ever. Everyone in the family and in his neighborhood knew whom to come to when anything needed fixing.

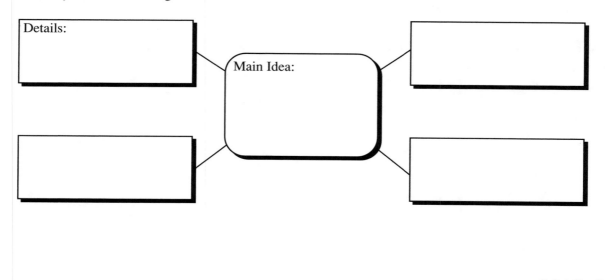

Details:

Main Idea:

2.   Stephen Foster composed songs, such as "My Old Kentucky Home," that we still sing today. Even though he was a talented writer of songs, he had a very unhappy life. He died at the age of 38, homeless, without friends, and almost penniless. In fact, he made very little money from any of the 200 songs he wrote.

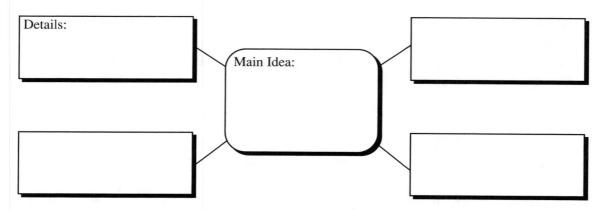

Details:

Main Idea:

Name _____ Date _____

What's the Big Idea?

Directions

Read each passage. Fill in the main idea and the supporting details.

1.   Manuel knew exactly what he had to do Saturday. He got up early and fixed his mom a breakfast fit for a queen. He waxed her car and cleaned his room without being told. When she left to go to the store, he hurried to the kitchen and baked her birthday cake. He carefully counted out the candles and stuck them into the icing. He knew she thought no one would remember her birthday. Had he done enough to make her day special?

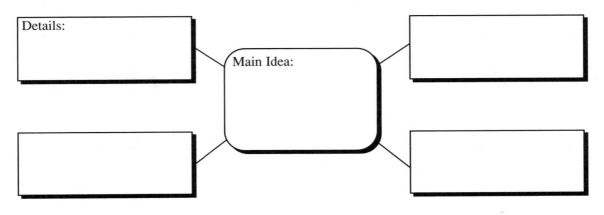

2.   The whale is often mistaken for a fish instead of a mammal. The whale breathes air, has hair on parts of its body, and is warm-blooded. Baby whales, called calves, get milk from their mother's body. These are all characteristics of mammals.

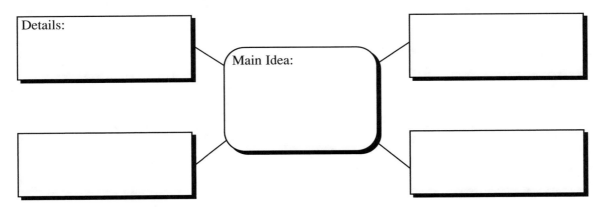

Name _____ Date _____

Get to the Point

Directions

Read each story. Fill in the main idea and the supporting details.

1. Roger had a collection of leaves that he had made in fourth grade. He also had a stamp collection and a terrific baseball card collection. Now, he was looking for coins minted the year he was born. The only collection that his parents had interfered with was when he was five and had started an ant collection. The ants had escaped and headed for the kitchen.

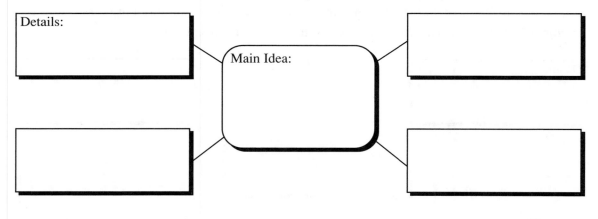

Details:

Main Idea:

2. Marcia pulled her scarf tighter around her face. Her toes felt numb inside her boots, and her fingers, curled inside their mittens, were losing all feeling, too. The wind pushed at her back, helping her on her way. Unfortunately, on the walk back home, she'd have to face that biting wind.

Details:

Main Idea:

Tool 5 · Summarizing

Preparation: Make copies of pages 25 (two sets) and 26. Make overheads of pages 24 and 25.

Anticipatory Set: Write five *W*s in a column on the board. Ask your students if they can identify the five words that start with a *W* that help ask five important questions. Then write out the words: *who*, *what*, *where*, *when*, and *why*.

Purpose: Tell the students that they are going to use these five words to help them summarize a passage. Explain that these are the five words that reporters use to get all of the information for their stories, and the students will be reporting on a passage.

Input: Define *summarizing* as telling the most important part of the story.

Modeling: Show the overhead, page 25. Show how the students are going to complete the five *W*'s to summarize. Then place the passage (page 24) on the overhead. Read the passage, and underline important information as you read. Then ask the students to help you identify the *who*, *what*, *where*, *when*, and *why* of the story. Pass out page 25 to all of the students. Have the students fill in the chart as you fill in the overhead chart.

Guided Practice: Explain that the students will now use this information to summarize the passage. They will combine the phrases and words from the five *W*s into three sentences. This will be the summary. Remind them to cross out what they use from the left column after they use it in a sentence. When they have used all of the information, remind them to proofread what they have written to make sure it makes sense.

Check for Understanding: Review the five *W*s. Then, have several students volunteer to read their summary. Cross off the information they use on the overhead chart to ensure that they used all of the information.

Independent Practice: Pass out page 26 and the second copy of page 25. Explain that the students will now read another passage and use the five *W*s to write a summary for the passage. Remind them to cross out the words they use from the left column when writing their summary.

Closure: Review the five *W*s. Have the students say what the five *W*s stand for. Then ask them how they can use the five *W*s in their everyday lives.

One More Night

The tent was up, and inside it, the sleeping bags were spread out on foam pads. The cooler was full of good things to eat, and a fire was all set for when they returned from their walk in the forest. It was a nice spot, surrounded by tall pines and hardwoods. The forest floor was covered with soft pine needles and leaves, and the scent of pine and balsam floated on the air. Bailey knew she should be appreciative of this chance to be here with her dad in the woods, but she could not seem to relax. He had been planning this weekend for months, but she had been dreading it for just as long.

Bailey liked being in her own house, sleeping in her own bed, cleaning up in her bathroom where there was hot running water, and eating bug-free at the kitchen table. Here, she would have to clean up in a river in which lived all manner of fish and other disagreeable water creatures, sleep in a tent in the dark in the middle of nowhere, and eat with the bugs. They would have to cook their own food over a campfire and wash the dishes in the river. It all seemed like too much work to Bailey, and the woods were scary, too. She tried not to betray her real feelings to her father; she didn't want to disappoint him, but this seemed like a nightmare!

Bailey and her father went for a walk before supper. It was very quiet in the woods, and their feet hardly made a sound on the soft carpet of needles. They saw a beaver that slapped its tail on the water and then dove underneath, leaving barely a ripple on the surface. They later saw him climb up the embankment on the far side of the river and disappear into the woods. They saw chipmunks and rabbits. A fox streaked by farther up the path. Boisterous jays scolded them for walking too near.

That evening after dinner, the sky was dotted with millions of shining stars. As the fire burned down to embers, the soft lapping of the water on the shore and the sound of the creatures in the woods were more comforting than ominous, as Bailey had expected. Her sleeping bag was soft and warm, and she woke to the sound of birds singing and the smell of bacon frying. In the fresh, early-morning air, she splashed her face with the clear river water. Today they were planning to break camp and head for home. She looked over at her father, cracking eggs into the frying pan and humming to himself. He seemed to be having fun; maybe she could convince him to stay for one more night.

Summary

Directions

Read the passage. Use the five *W*s to compile information. Then write a summary using the information.

WHO:

WHAT:

WHERE:

WHEN:

WHY:

SUMMARY:

Name _____ Date _____

Burglar Bungle

Jerry never forgot the day they had all the excitement at their house. It was a Sunday afternoon. Jerry's dad, a police officer, was at work driving his squad car. Jerry's mom had taken his little sisters and his grandmother to the afternoon movies. Jerry was more interested in being out with his friends than going to the movies.

In the middle of the afternoon, Jerry returned home to get some money. While he was looking for his extra cash, he heard noises upstairs. Jerry thought the noises sounded like drawers opening and closing. "That's funny," he mused. "I thought everyone was out." So he went to the bottom of the stairs and called, "Who's up there?" There was no response. He called again. Nothing.

At this point Jerry decided that he had a problem. If burglars were upstairs, he was not inclined to go up and confront them. So he ran outside, leaving the front door open, and rushed next door to the Danners' house. On hearing his problem, Mr. Danner called the police. Then, armed with a baseball bat, he accompanied Jerry back to the house.

Meanwhile, the call about the burglar was radioed to Jerry's dad's squad car. "What's going on?" he cried to his partner. "That's my house! Move it!"

By the time the squad car reached the house, Mr. Danner was just coming downstairs, dragging his bat and looking annoyed. Jerry followed, a sheepish grin on his face. "It's all right!" he called, seeing his dad rush up the walk.

"It was just Grandma," Jerry explained when everyone had gathered in the entryway. "She didn't go with Mom and the girls to the movies. Instead, she came over here to pack up some things for Mom to take to Goodwill. She had her hearing aid turned down and didn't hear a thing when I called upstairs!"

So everything had turned out all right after all. Jerry's dad was relieved, and Jerry had a good story to tell his mom when she returned. The only disgruntled member of the "rescue team" was Mr. Danner, who had sincerely wanted to catch a burglar and be on the six o'clock news.

Lesson Plans Using Graphic Organizers 6, SV 2074-5

Tool 6 Understanding Narrative Poetry

Preparation: Make copies of pages 29 and 30. Make an overhead of page 28.

Anticipatory Set: Ask the students if they can define the word *narrative*. Allow several students to predict what the definition is, and then have them use words like *narrate* and *narrator* to help explain the meaning.

Purpose: Explain that narratives tell stories. A narrative poem is a poem that tells a story. Give an example of a narrative ("The Night Before Christmas," Dr. Seuss stories, etc.).

Input: Explain that narrative poems tell stories using lyrics and stanzas. Explain that sometimes a narrative poem is really long, and other times it can be very short. No matter the length, the poem tells a story.

Modeling: Place page 28 on the overhead. With the students, read the information box and the narrative poem. Discuss the story told in the poem. Ask the students to identify whom the poem was about and tell what he did. Then ask a student to tell you what the poem was mostly about. Then complete the chart on the bottom of the page together. Ask for volunteers to identify the characters, setting, and the plot of the narrative poem.

Guided Practice: Pass out page 29. Explain that the students are going to read another poem with a partner. As they read the poem, they are to identify what the narrative poem is about. They will discuss the poem and its story. After they read it, the whole group will discuss the poem.

Check for Understanding: As a whole group, discuss some of the events in the poem. Have several students volunteer what they found in the poem. Review what the definition of *narrative* is, and ask how this pertains to the poem.

Independent Practice: Now that the students are aware of the narrative aspects of the poem, they will identify the characters, setting, and plot of the poem. They will reread the poem and complete the graphic organizer on page 30 independently.

Closure: Review the purpose of narrative poems. Ask the students to think about why narrative poems were used to convey important events in history. Discuss the importance of narrative poems during times of high illiteracy. Then discuss other reasons a poet may choose to write a narrative poem, and invite the students to write one of their own.

Name _____ Date _____

A Narrative Poem

In a narrative poem, a writer tells a story. Like all stories, a narrative poem has a plot, a setting, and characters. In addition, it contains figures of speech and rhyme and rhythm.

Paul Revere's Ride
[excerpt]

Listen, my children, and you shall hear
Of the midnight ride of Paul Revere,
On the eighteenth of April, in seventy-five;
Hardly a man is now alive
Who remembers that famous day and year.
He said to his friend, "If the British march,
By land or sea from the town tonight,
Hang a lantern aloft in the belfry arch
Of the North Church tower as a signal light,—
One, if by land, and two, if by sea;
And I on the opposite shore will be,
Ready to ride and spread the alarm
Through every Middlesex village and farm,
For the country folk to be up and to arm."

—Henry Wadsworth Longfellow

Directions

Complete the diagram using information from the example.

Characters	Setting	Plot

Looking for Trouble

"Who is it you'll be with today
when you go down to the park to play?
What's his name?" I heard Father say.

"Yeah, whatshisname. You know. That guy."
When I talk to Dad I never lie.
I wouldn't even want to try.

"Did you say Billy Beanalee?"
Now Dad was looking straight at me,
and I nodded yes. "Oh, no! not he!"

"Not that rascal!" Father said.
"You'll come home injured, or, worse yet, dead!"
He was holding and shaking his head.

"He's not a good influence, that boy!
There's not a soul he can't annoy,"
Dad said. "He's too clever, and he's coy!"

So I left my father in a worried way
and went off to join my friend in play.
I was late, and Billy had come halfway.

"I bet they lectured you back there,"
he said. "But gosh, it isn't fair
that I get more trouble than my share."

"Let's just sit," he said. "Not do a thing
and hope that my luck doesn't bring
us trouble … or boredom … or anything."

He twiddled his thumbs, gave a yawn or two,
then said, "I'll tell you what we'll do.
I'll find trouble and run it off for you!"

Narrative Poetry

Directions

Read the narrative poem. Complete the chart using the information in the poem.

Title of the poem: _____

Characters:

Settings:

Plot:

Tool 7 Defining Prefixes

Preparation: Make copies of pages 33 and 34. Make an overhead of page 32.

Anticipatory Set: Write the word *write* on the board. Ask a student to define the word or explain what it means. Then add the prefix *re-* to the word, and ask another student what the new word means. Then ask for a volunteer to explain what those two letters did to the meaning of the word.

Purpose: Explain that the students will be using *prefixes* to change the meanings of words. They will also determine the definitions of the new words.

Input: Explain that the two letters are a prefix. Explain that *prefixes* are added to words to change the meaning of the word.

Modeling: Place page 32 on the overhead. Read the definition and the examples of *prefixes*. Read their meanings and how they affect the words to which they are added. Do the practice exercise with the students by reading the clue in the parentheses and having them choose the word that fits the description.

Guided Practice: Pass out page 33. Explain that the students are going to work with partners on another activity. They will use the dictionary to help them look up words with the given prefix. Then, using those words, the students will try to define the prefix.

Check for Understanding: After a given amount of time, refocus the students. Ask for volunteers to read the three words they found for the first prefix. Then have a student define the meaning of that prefix and its effect on the words.

Independent Practice: After reviewing the function of prefixes, pass out page 34. Explain that the students will do the same process for finding the meanings and examples for this set of prefixes. However, they will complete these independently.

Closure: Review the purposes of prefixes. Have a student tell what adding a prefix does to a word. Then ask the students to explain how this information will help them in their daily activities.

Name _____ Date _____

Good Beginnings

A **prefix** is a syllable or syllables added to the beginning of a word to change its meaning. A **base word** is a word to which other word parts may be added.

Prefix	Meaning	New Word
com, con	with	companion
dis	away, off, lack of, not	displease
ex	former	ex-mayor
extra	outside of, beyond	extraordinary
fore	before, in front of, ahead	foreground
il	not (often before *l*)	illegal
im	not (often before *m*)	immature
in	not	incomplete
ir	not (often before *r*)	irregular
mis	badly, wrong, not	misunderstand
non	not	nonsense
over	too much, over	overeat
pre	before	preheat
re	back, again	retrace
un	not	unclear
un	the opposite of	unlock

Directions

Read each sentence. Replace the words in parentheses ( ) with a word that has the same meaning. Each word should begin with one of the prefixes from the list above.

1. People have accomplished (beyond the ordinary) _____ things.

2. Harriet Tubman brought more than 300 slaves out of the South, and she never (led badly) _____ one of them.

3. Louis Pasteur worked hard to (come over) _____ rabies.

4. Robert Goddard was (not content) _____ until he proved that rockets could fly with liquid fuel.

5. Elizabeth Kenny showed great (sight ahead) _____ in her plans for helping polio victims to (gain back) _____ their strength.

Name _____ Date _____

Prefixes and Their Meanings

Directions

Use a dictionary to find three examples of words with the stated prefix. Then write the meaning of the prefix in the box.

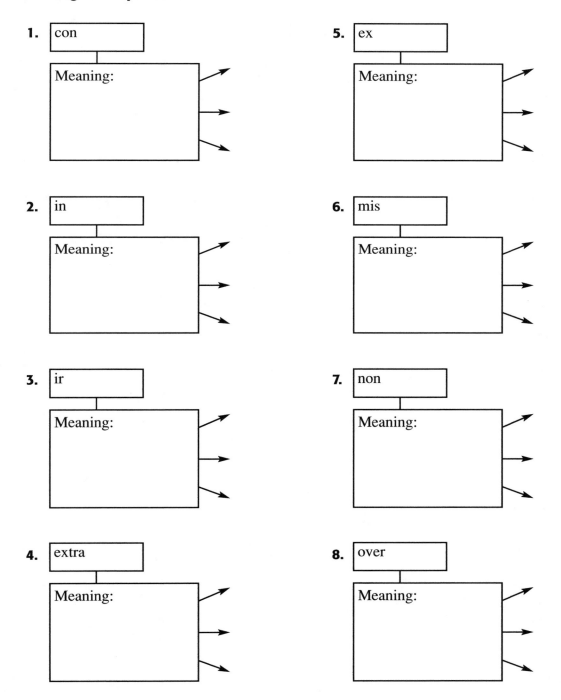

1. con

Meaning:

2. in

Meaning:

3. ir

Meaning:

4. extra

Meaning:

5. ex

Meaning:

6. mis

Meaning:

7. non

Meaning:

8. over

Meaning:

Name _____ Date _____

More Prefixes and Their Meanings

Directions

Use a dictionary to find three examples of words with the stated prefix. Then write the meaning of the prefix in the box.

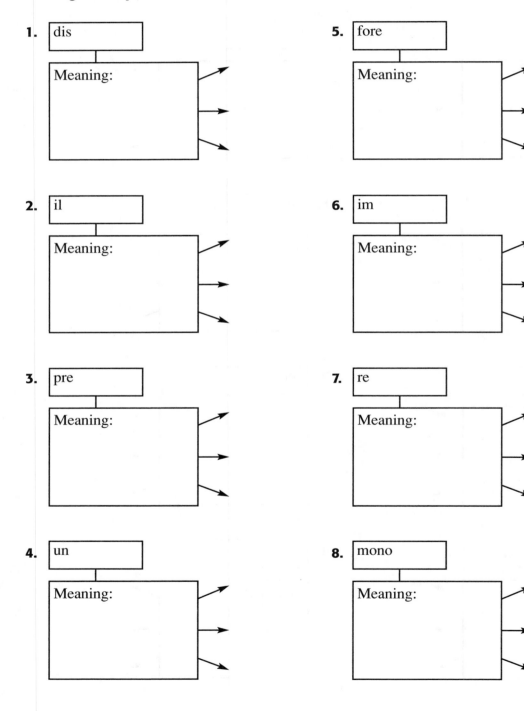

1. dis

Meaning:

2. il

Meaning:

3. pre

Meaning:

4. un

Meaning:

5. fore

Meaning:

6. im

Meaning:

7. re

Meaning:

8. mono

Meaning:

Tool 8 Problem Solving with Fractions

Preparation: Copy pages 37 and 38 for students. Make page 36 an overhead.

Anticipatory Set: Ask the students if they have ever had the dilemma of having a pizza with too few pieces for the number of people. Ask them what they could do to solve the problem.

Purpose: Explain that the students will use fractions to solve problems. Explain that they will also need to draw pictures to help them solve these problems.

Input: Explain that the students will read the problems carefully and determine which functions to use. They will then draw pictures and solve the problems.

Modeling: Place page 36 on the overhead. Read the information at the top of the page. Read through the process of solving the problem. Show how drawing the picture helps to solve the problem. Then, work through the four problems. Talk through the process and steps.

Guided Practice: Divide the class into partners. Pass out page 37. Have the partners read through the activity and ask any questions prior to beginning. Then, read the directions out loud, and have the students work on the two problems together.

Check for Understanding: Remind the students that drawing pictures helps to solve the problems. Ask for one set of partners to describe the process they used to solve the first problem. Ask if any group worked the problem differently. Then, have another set of partners describe how they did the second problem. Check to make sure that everyone is drawing pictures and has an understanding of how to determine the process of the problem.

Independent Practice: Pass out page 38. Have the students read over the page to see if they have any questions. Then have them work independently on the assignment.

Closure: Review the strategies they learned for solving word problems. Remind them that drawing pictures is helpful. Ask students if they can think of any other real world instance in which they may need to solve a problem using fractions.

Name _____ Date _____

Cheerful Candy Stripers

> Sometimes a drawing helps to organize the information in a problem.
> Be sure to include all the important facts in a drawing.

Directions

Read the problem.

Three candy stripers visited the hospital's elderly patients. They divided their time evenly so each would have a turn. Altogether, they worked for a total of $5\frac{2}{5}$ hours. How much time did each candy striper spend with elderly patients?

Identify the facts.

There were 3 candy stripers. They divided their time evenly. They worked a total of $5\frac{2}{5}$ hours.

Make a drawing.

Each box is divided into fifths.
Each box represents 1 hour.

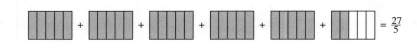

Solve the problem.

Divide the boxes into 3 equal groups. Circle each group. Altogether, there are 27 fifths, or $\frac{27}{5}$. There are 3 groups. So each group contains $\frac{9}{5}$. $\frac{9}{5} = 1\frac{4}{5}$ Each candy striper worked $1\frac{4}{5}$ hours.

Now it's your turn! Make a drawing to help you solve each problem.

1. For a snack, the 3 candy stripers ate $3\frac{3}{4}$ ounces of carrots. If they shared the carrots equally, how many ounces of carrots did each candy striper eat?

   _____

2. The 3 candy stripers pooled their money and bought $7\frac{1}{3}$ dozen flowers from the gift shop. If they divided the flowers equally among 4 patients, how many dozen flowers did each patient get?

   _____

3. How many flowers did each patient get?

   _____

4. If the candy stripers used $4\frac{4}{5}$ sheets of paper to write notes about 6 patients, how many sheets did they use for each patient?

   _____

Unit 2: Math

Lesson Plans Using Graphic Organizers 6, SV 2074-5

Name _____ Date _____

A Multicultural Feast

> Some problems give too many facts. If there are too many facts, cross out the extra facts. Then work the problem.

Directions

Read the problem.

Sharona worked in the hospital. She asked everyone to bring something for the multicultural party. She brought $6\frac{2}{3}$ packages of rice cakes and $4\frac{7}{8}$ pounds of tofu. If she divided the packages of rice cakes by $\frac{1}{3}$ to make more packages, how many smaller packages of rice cakes would she have?

Identify the facts you need and don't need.

Need: Sharona brought $6\frac{2}{3}$ packages of rice cakes.

Need: She divided the packages of rice cakes by $\frac{1}{3}$.

Don't need: She brought $4\frac{7}{8}$ pounds of tofu.

Solve the problem.

Change the mixed number into an improper fraction: $6\frac{2}{3} = \frac{20}{3}$. Invert the second fraction (divisor) to find the reciprocal: $\frac{1}{3}$ becomes $\frac{3}{1}$. To divide, multiply the improper fraction by the reciprocal. Reduce the answer. $\frac{20}{3} \times \frac{3}{1} = \frac{60}{3} = 20$ She would have 20 smaller packages of rice cakes.

Now it's your turn! Cross out the extra facts. Then solve the problems.

1.   Mr. Olson brought Swedish meatballs to the party. He bought 2 pounds of beef. His recipe makes $9\frac{1}{2}$ large meatballs. If he divides the number of meatballs by $\frac{1}{4}$, he will have enough smaller meatballs for everyone. How many smaller meatballs can he make?

_____

2.   Simone made Greek baklava for the party. She used $\frac{1}{2}$ cup of nuts and $\frac{3}{4}$ cup of honey in the recipe. She cut 10 pieces from 1 pan. If she divided the pieces by $\frac{1}{3}$, how many slices would she have?

_____

Everyday Hospital Tasks

Some problems do not tell you to add, subtract, multiply, or divide.
Read the problem carefully to help you to choose the correct operation.

Directions

Read the problem.

Pat has $15\frac{2}{5}$ yards of gauze to make bandages. Each bandage uses $1\frac{2}{5}$ yards. How many bandages can Pat make?

Identify the facts.

Pat has $15\frac{2}{5}$ yards of gauze. Each bandage uses $1\frac{2}{5}$ yards of gauze.

Choose an operation.

Divide $15\frac{2}{5}$ by $1\frac{2}{5}$ to find the number of bandages Pat can make.

Solve the problem.

$15\frac{2}{5} \div 1\frac{2}{5} = \frac{77}{5} \div \frac{7}{5} = \frac{77}{5} \times \frac{5}{7} = \frac{385}{35} = 11$

Now it's your turn! Choose an operation to solve each problem.

1. Pat has $56\frac{1}{4}$ pounds of plaster. If 1 cast uses $3\frac{3}{4}$ pounds of plaster, how many casts can Pat make?

    _____

2. Pat can wrap a bandage with $1\frac{1}{10}$ yards of tape. If she has $8\frac{4}{5}$ yards of tape, how many bandages can she wrap?

    _____

3. The nursery uses $2\frac{1}{4}$ packages of cotton balls every day. There are $13\frac{1}{2}$ packages on the shelf. How many days' supply of cotton balls does the nursery have?

    _____

4. The emergency room uses $9\frac{3}{4}$ times more cotton balls in a month than the nursery uses in a day. If the nursery uses $2\frac{2}{3}$ packages in a day, how many packages does the emergency room use in a month?

    _____

Tool 9 — Finding the Circumference and Area

Preparation: Copy pages 41 and 42 for students. Make page 40 an overhead. Bring a round hat box.

Anticipatory Set: Tell the students that you want to wrap the hat box. But you don't have a lot of wrapping paper, so you want to make sure that you have enough before you begin wrapping. Ask the students to tell you how they would determine if you had enough paper to wrap the box.

Purpose: Explain that circles can have a circumference and an area. The students will solve problems to find the circumference and area of circles.

Input: Define *circumference* as the distance around the circle. The formula for finding the circumference is $C = \pi D$. Define *diameter* as the line between two points on the circumference that passes through the center of the circle. Then, define the *area* as the space inside the circle. The formula to find the area is $A = \pi r^2$. Define r as the radius, or the distance from the center of the circle to the edge.

Modeling: Place page 40 on the overhead. Read through the information with the students. Show the pictures of the radius and diameter. Then work through the sample problem. Show how to substitute a given number in the formula. Explain that π equals approximately 3.14. Tell the students to use 3.14 as the value of π when they solve these problems.

Guided Practice: Divide the students into partners. Pass out page 41. Explain that the students are going to solve these problems using the formulas for circumference and area.

Check for Understanding: Review the definitions of *circumference*, *area*, *diameter*, and *radius*. Then go over the problems on page 41. Have different students explain which formula they used to solve the problem, how they worked it, and their answer.

Independent Practice: Pass out page 42. Have the students read over the page to see if they have any questions. Then have them work independently on the assignment. Remind them to use the correct formulas to solve the problems.

Closure: Review the formulas for circumference and area of circles. Ask the students if they can think of any reasons they may need to use the formula for the circumference or area of a circle.

Round and Round We Go!

To find the circumference of a circle, use the formula $C = \pi D$. In the formula, D is the diameter of the circle. The diameter is a line between two points on the circumference, or the outer edge of a circle. The diameter passes through the center of the circle. The π in the formula is equal to 3.14.

To find the area of a circle, use the formula $A = \pi r^2$. The radius, or r, is the distance from the center of the circle to the circumference. The radius is equal to $\frac{1}{2}$ of the diameter.

HINT—The little 2 by the r means to square the number, or multiply it by itself.

Directions

Read the problem.

Find the circumference and area of a circle with a diameter of 8 inches.

Identify the facts.

The circle's diameter is 8 inches.

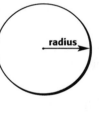

Use a formula.

To find the circumference of a circle, the formula is $C = \pi D$.
To find the area of a circle, the formula is $A = \pi r^2$.

Solve the problem.

To find the circumference:

$\pi = 3.14$ $D = 8$ $C = 3.14 \times 8 = 25.12$

The circumference is 25.12 inches.

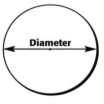

To find the area:

$\pi = 3.14$ $r = \frac{1}{2} \times D = \frac{1}{2} \times 8 = 4$ $r^2 = 4 \times 4 = 16$
$A = 3.14 \times 16 = 50.24$

The area is 50.24 square inches.

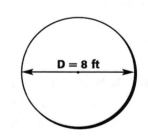

Unit 2: Math

Lesson Plans Using Graphic Organizers 6, SV 2074-5

Name _____ Date _____

More Circles

Circumference is the distance around a circle. The formula to find the *circumference* is $C = \pi D$, or *circumference* = π (pi, or 3.14) × *diameter*. The formula to find the *area* of a circle is $A = \pi r^2$, or *area* = π × *radius* × *radius*. Area is expressed in square units, such as square meters.

Directions

Find the circumference. Use 3.14 for π. Round to the nearest whole number.

1. diameter = 14 in.

_____

2. diameter = 42 mm

_____

3. radius = 14 in.

_____

4. radius = 7 cm

_____

Find the circumference. Use 3.14 for π. Round your answer to the nearest tenth. You may want to use a calculator.

5.

3 m

_____

6.

12 m

_____

7.

18 mm

_____

8. diameter = 4 cm

_____

9. diameter = 9 in.

_____

10. radius = 15 m

_____

Find the area of the circle. Use 3.14 for π. Round to the nearest tenth.

11. r = 10 in.

_____

12. D = 8 in.

_____

13. r = 5 m

_____

14. D = 6 ft

_____

15. r = 1.5 in.

_____

16. D = 6.4 cm

_____

17. r = 0.9 m

_____

18. r = 14.4 in.

_____

© Steck-Vaughn Company

Unit 2: Math
Lesson Plans Using Graphic Organizers 6, SV 2074-5

Name _____ Date _____

Circle Problems

To find the *circumference* of a circle, use the formula $C = \pi D$. In the formula, D is the diameter of the circle. The diameter is a line between two points on the circumference, or the outer edge of a circle. The diameter passes through the center of the circle. The π in the formula is equal to 3.14.

To find the area of a circle, use the formula $A = \pi r^2$. The radius, or r, is the distance from the center of the circle to the circumference. The radius is equal to $\frac{1}{2}$ of the diameter.

HINT—The little 2 by the r means to square the number, or multiply it by itself.

Directions

Answer the questions below.

1. The diameter of a circle is 18 inches. What is the radius?

_____

2. A wheel has a diameter of 14 inches. What is the circumference of the wheel?

_____

3. An apple pie has a radius of 5 inches. What is the area of the pie?

_____

4. If you cut the pie into 8 pieces, what part of the circumference will each piece be?

_____

5. A circle has a radius of 6 inches. What is the circumference?

_____

6. A circle has a diameter of 16 inches. What is the area of the circle?

_____

7. A small pizza has a diameter of 8 inches. A large pizza has a diameter of 14 inches. What is the difference in area between the large pizza and the small pizza?

_____

8. A tabletop has a circumference of 188.4 inches. What is the radius of this round tabletop?

_____

Unit 2: Math
Lesson Plans Using Graphic Organizers 6, SV 2074-5

Tool 10   Finding the Surface Area and Volume

Preparation: Copy pages 45 and 46 for students. Make page 44 an overhead. Gather several medium-sized boxes of various sizes, as well as several boxes and rulers for each student.

Anticipatory Set: Ask your students what information they would need to know if they wanted to cover one of the boxes with paper. Show them a box, and have the students discuss what information they would need to know. Then, ask them what they would need to know if you wanted to fill that box with cotton balls.

Purpose: Explain that the students would need to know the surface area and the volume to get that information.

Input: Define *surface area* as the combined area of the top and bottom, the two sides, and the front and back. To find the area of each side, they must multiply the length by the height. Then, they add the area of all the sides together. The *volume* of the rectangular shape can be found by multiplying the length, width, and height of the rectangle.

Modeling: Place page 44 on the overhead. Read through the information with the students. Show the model of the rectangular object. Point out the six surfaces. Then, work through the sample problem. Show how to substitute a given number in the formula. Work through the two sample problems together. Then, explain how they would find the volume for that shape. Model how to set up the equations, how to substitute the numbers, and how to solve the equation.

Guided Practice: Divide the students into partners. Pass out page 45. The students will find the volume for these rectangular objects. Review the equation for volume.

Check for Understanding: Review the definitions and equations of *surface area* and *volume*. Then, go over the volume problems.

Independent Practice: Explain that the students are now going to apply what they know about surface area and volume to real rectangular objects. Explain that the students are going to go to different stations that have a box at each one. At each station, they will measure the boxes to find the surface area and the volume. They will use rulers to help them solve the problems. Pass out page 46. Have the students read over the page to see if they have any questions. Then, have them work independently on the assignment. Remind them to use the correct formulas to solve the problems.

Closure: Review the formulas for surface area and volume. Ask the students if they can think of any real world examples of how they could apply the process of finding the surface area or volume.

Name _____   Date _____

Three-dimensional Problems

A *three-dimensional* figure has width, depth, and height. An example is a box. On a rectangular box, there are 6 surface areas, or faces. The top and bottom are the same size in area, the front and back are the same size, and the remaining 2 sides are the same size. To find the total surface area of the box, you must find the area of the top, the front, and a side. Add these areas, then multiply by 2 to find the area of all 6 faces.

Directions

Read the problem.
Find the total surface area of a rectangular box with these dimensions in inches: W = 4; H = 2, L = 3.

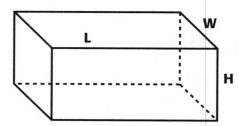

Make a plan.
First, you must find the area of the top, the front, and a side. Then, add the 3 areas. Then, multiply by 2.

Solve the problem.
Find the areas.
Top A = 4 × 3 = 12 square inches
Front A = 4 × 2 = 8 square inches
Side A = 3 × 2 = 6 square inches
Add the areas. 12 + 8 + 6 = 26 square inches
Then multiply by 2. 26 × 2 = 52 square inches.
The rectangular box has a total surface area of 52 square inches.

Now it's your turn! Make a plan, then solve these problems.

1.   A rectangular box is 8 inches wide, 10 inches long, and 4 inches high. What is the total surface area of the box?

_____

2.   A square box (also called a cube) has a height of 5 inches. What is the total surface area of the cube?

_____

Name _____ Date _____

Volume

The *volume* is the measure of the interior of a three-dimensional figure. *Volume* is expressed in cubic units, such as cubic inches. The formula to find the *volume* of a rectangular prism is $V = l \times w \times h$, or *volume = length × width × height*.

Directions

Answer the questions below.

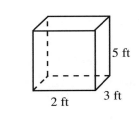

1. What dimensions do you need to know to find the volume of a rectangular prism? _____

2. How can you find the volume using these dimensions? _____

3. Suppose the dimensions of a rectangular prism are given in inches. In what units do you express the volume? _____

Tell what numbers to multiply to find the volume of the rectangular prism.

4.

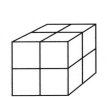

_____

5.

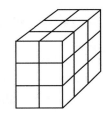

_____

6.

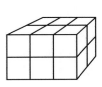

_____

Find the volume.

7.

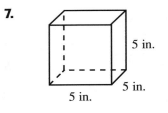

_____

8.

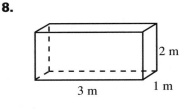

_____

9.

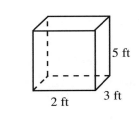

_____

Surface Area and Volume of Boxes

Directions

Measure the width, length, and height of the box at each station.
Use that information to find the surface area and the volume.

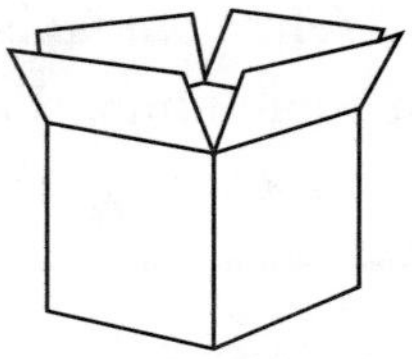

1. width _____

length _____

height _____

Surface Area:
    Formula: _____
    Answer: _____
Volume:
    Formula: _____
    Answer: _____

2. width _____

length _____

height _____

Surface Area:
    Formula: _____
    Answer: _____
Volume:
    Formula: _____
    Answer: _____

3. width _____

length _____

height _____

Surface Area:
    Formula: _____
    Answer: _____
Volume:
    Formula: _____
    Answer: _____

4. width _____

length _____

height _____

Surface Area:
    Formula: _____
    Answer: _____
Volume:
    Formula: _____
    Answer: _____

5. width _____

length _____

height _____

Surface Area:
    Formula: _____
    Answer: _____
Volume:
    Formula: _____
    Answer: _____

Tool 11) Finding the Mean, Mode, and Median

Preparation: Make copies of pages 49 and 50. Make an overhead of page 48.

Anticipatory Set: Ask the students if they know how a baseball player's batting average is determined. Then explain that it is the number of times a player hit the ball divided by the number of times the player tried to hit the ball. Ask the students if they can think of any other things that get averaged.

Purpose: Explain that the students are going to find the mean, mode, and median of several numbers.

Input: Define *mean* as the average of a set of numbers, the *mode* as the number that occurs the most often in a set, and the *median* as the middle number in a set of numbers ordered from least to greatest.

Modeling: Place page 48 on the overhead. Review how to find the average using the sum of the numbers divided by the number of addends. Show how to manipulate the equation so that the students can solve the equation for any missing part. Work through the five problems as a whole group.

Guided Practice: Divide the class into partners. Pass out page 49. Read the definition of *mode*, and read over the rest of the given information. Then ask the students to work through the problems and answer them using the chart.

Check for Understanding: Review the definition of *mode*. Then ask the students to share their answers. Ask them to explain how they solved the problems and to explain their answers.

Independent Practice: Review the definition of *mean* and *mode*. Explain that the students will now explore finding the median. Explain the definition of *median* as an ordered set of numbers from least to greatest, with the median as the middle number. Explain that if there is an even set of numbers, the students will have to find the average of the middle two numbers. Have the students work independently on the problems.

Closure: Review the definitions of *mean*, *mode*, and *median*. Ask the students to think of real world situations in which they might need to find the mean, mode, or median.

Name _____   Date _____

They Play Mean!

Remember, to find the average, or mean, of a set of numbers, add all of the numbers and divide the sum by the number of addends.

In baseball, a player's batting average is the number of times the player hit the ball safely divided by the number of times the player tried to hit the ball. The number is represented in thousandths for greater accuracy. For example, when a batter has 50 attempts (at-bats) and gets 17 hits, the player's average is $\frac{17}{50}$, or .340.

Directions

Answer the questions below.

1. When a batter has 12 hits in 50 at-bats, what is the batter's batting average?

_____

2. If a batter has an average of .420 after 50 at-bats, how many balls did the player hit?

_____

3. The same batter's average drops to .400 after 25 more at-bats. How many balls out of the 25 did the batter hit?

_____

4. How many balls out of the 75 at-bats did the player miss?

_____

There are a few players who can hit the ball from both right-handed and left-handed stances. These batters are called switch-hitters. Switch-hitters keep averages for both sides to see from which side they bat better. A batter might hit 30% left-handed and 35% right-handed. The player's total batting average is $\frac{.300 + .350}{2}$, or .325.

5. A switch-hitter is batting .320 right-handed after 50 at-bats. The batter hits 20 out of 50 balls hitting left-handed. What is the total batting average?

_____

Name _____ Date _____

Tennis Is the Mode

> The mode is the number that occurs the most often in a set of numbers.

Don is a member of the Net Set Tennis Club.
He makes a table to show the age of each member and the
number of years each person has played.

The Net Set Tennis Club

Name	Years Played	Age	Name	Years Played	Age
Lee	4	14	Keisha	1	9
Mark	2	13	Don	5	12
Lynn	5	12	Daniel	2	14
Terri	1	9	Sherry	3	10
Melissa	4	14	Jim	5	13
Greg	5	12	Luis	3	12

Directions

Use the table to answer the questions below.

1. Write all the ages of the tennis players
   from the greatest to the least.

   _____

   _____

2. Which number occurs most often?

   _____

3. Write all the years the members have
   played from the least to the greatest.

   _____

   _____

4. Which number occurs most often?

   _____

5. When could knowing the mode of a set of
   numbers be useful to people who keep data?

   _____

   _____

   _____

Name _____ Date _____

Trash in the Median

To find the median number, order a set of numbers from the least to greatest. The middle number is the median number. If there is an even amount of numbers, then you find the mean of the middle two numbers.

The table shows the recycling materials and their weights that the students in Mr. Ito's class collected in five weeks.

Weight of Recycling Materials

	Week 1	Week 2	Week 3	Week 4	Week 5
Cans	45 lb.	42 lb.	60 lb.	60 lb.	50 lb.
Glass	55 lb.	42 lb.	28 lb.	35 lb.	38 lb.
Newspaper	67 lb.	59 lb.	70 lb.	62 lb.	65 lb.
Plastic	21 lb.	13 lb.	11 lb.	19 lb.	9 lb.

Directions

Use the table to answer the questions below.

1. Write all the weights of the recyclable materials collected during week 3 from the least to the greatest. What is the median number?

   _____

   _____

2. What is the median number for the weight of all of the materials collected in week 1?

   _____

3. What is the median number for the weight of all of the plastic collected?

   _____

4. What is the median number for the weight of all of the cans collected?

   _____

5. How could data about the median weight be used by a recycling company?

   _____

   _____

Unit 2: Math
Lesson Plans Using Graphic Organizers 6, SV 2074-5

Tool 12 Using a Logic Table

Preparation: Copy pages 53 and 54 for students. Make page 52 an overhead.

Anticipatory Set: Show the students the overhead sheet. Read only the problem, and ask the students to solve the problem. Ask them why it is difficult to solve the problem. After they give reasons, ask if anyone has a suggestion as to what could be used to organize the information to solve the problem.

Purpose: Show the chart. Then explain that the students are going to use logic and a chart to solve word problems.

Input: Define *logic* as reasonableness and good guessing. Explain that using a chart will help organize the information.

Modeling: Go over the example on the overhead. Proceed step by step, explaining how you know where to place an X. Show how the answer appears after you use the information given to weed out the wrong answers. Have a student restate your reasoning after each step to ensure that the students understand the process.

Guided Practice: Explain the directions for practice page 53. Divide the class into partners. Have them work the two problems and discuss how they got their answers with their partners.

Check for Understanding: Review the process of solving logic problems with a chart. Then reread the problem, and have the partners volunteer to give the answers for the problems.

Independent Practice: Read the directions for page 54. Point out the charts, and remind the students to use the top row and side row for items and names. Monitor the students as they work independently.

Closure: Refocus the students on the overhead sheet. Review the steps to work a logic word problem.

Name _____ Date _____

Logic Tables

Directions

Complete each logic table. Eliminate a box by drawing an X, and place an 0 in each box that is correct.

1. Louis, Patricia, Emanuel, and Jacqueline like to swim, fly kites, read, and play chess. Each person favors one hobby the most. Find each person's favorite.

    a. No person's name has the same number of letters as his or her favorite hobby.
    b. The person who likes chess the most is a girl and is friends with both Louis and Patricia.
    c. The person who likes reading the most is a boy.

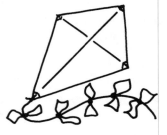

You can use a **logic table** to help you find the answers. On the table, you eliminate a box by putting an *X* in it, and you put an *0* in each box that is correct. For example, Louis's name has the same number of letters as *chess*. Statement **a** tells you that *chess* cannot be Louis's favorite.

	Jacqueline	Patricia	Louis	Emanuel
Chess			X	
Reading				
Swimming				
Kite flying				

2. Eyes, Ears, Nose, and Hands were secret agents. Their mission was to investigate Colonel Grabbit, who was an enemy agent. They went to his house during a party. One spy was disguised as a butler in the sitting room, one as a chef at the outdoor barbecue, and one as a coat rack in the foyer; one hid in the fountain on the lawn. Use this information to determine which was which.

    a. Eyes later said it was hard to hold still for so long.
    b. Ears went over and whispered to Hands during the party.
    c. Hands said he envied Nose and Eyes for being indoors.

	Eyes	Ears	Nose	Hands
Coat Rack				
Chef				
Butler				
Fountain				

More Logic Tables

Directions

Complete each logic table. Eliminate a box by drawing an *X*, and place an *0* in each box that is correct.

1.   David, Laurinda, Angela, and Lynn like to dive, ride motorcycles, fly kites, and play tennis. Among these hobbies, each person favors a different one. Use the table to find each person's favorite.

   a. No person's name has the same number of letters as his or her favorite hobby.

   b. The person who likes to dive the most is a girl and is friends with both Laurinda and Angela.

   c. The person who likes to ride motorcycles the most has a mustache.

	Lynn	Angela	David	Laurinda
Diving				
Motorcycles				
Tennis				
Kite flying				

2.   Mr. Ho, Mr. Liang, Mr. Morozumi, Mr. Lee, and Mr. Perry are cooks. At a recent food auction,

   a. each cook had a casserole for sale.

   b. no one bought a casserole baked by her own husband.

   c. Mr. Ho's casserole was bought by Mrs. Liang.

   d. Mr. Lee's casserole was bought by the woman whose husband's casserole was bought by Mrs. Morozumi.

   e. Mrs. Ho bought the casserole baked by the husband of the woman who bought Mr. Perry's casserole.

   f. Mrs. Lee bought a casserole from someone who has her same initials.

Complete the table to indicate who bought each cook's casserole. (HINT: Think of clues in terms of unknowns. For example, clue d: Mrs. X bought Mr. Lee's casserole; Mrs. Morozumi bought Mr. X's casserole.)

	Mr. Ho	Mr. Liang	Mr. Morozumi	Mr. Lee	Mr. Perry
Mrs. Ho					
Mrs. Liang					
Mrs. Morozumi					
Mrs. Lee					
Mrs. Perry					

Name _____ Date _____

Using Logic to Solve Problems

Directions

Complete each logic table. Place an *X* in the boxes you eliminate and an *0* in the box with the correct answer.

1.   Mr. Washington, Mr. Forrest, Mr. Perrotti, Mr. Li, and Mr. Clark are bakers. At a recent cake sale

   a. each baker had a cake for sale.
   b. no one bought a cake baked by her husband.
   c. Mr. Washington's cake was bought by Mrs. Forrest.
   d. Mr. Li's cake was bought by the woman whose husband's cake was bought by Mrs. Perrotti.
   e. Mrs. Washington bought the cake baked by the husband of the woman who bought Mr. Clark's cake.
   f. Mr. Forrest and Mr. Li made strawberry cakes. Mrs. Washington is allergic to strawberries.

Use the table to indicate who bought each man's cake.

	Mr. Washington	Mr. Forrest	Mr. Perrotti	Mr. Li	Mr. Clark
Mrs. Washington					
Mrs. Forrest					
Mrs. Perrotti					
Mrs. Li					
Mrs. Clark					

2.   Five spies from different countries were spying on each other. One Thursday, they were in various spots in an art museum. In the diagram at the right, the letters refer to spaces occupied by spies. The arrows indicate which spy or spies each man could see. You also know these facts.

   a. Ax could see two other spies, while Rat could see only one.
   b. Flea was watched by only one spy, who was watched by two.
   c. Jam could be seen only by Flea.
   d. Gum was seen by both Ax and Jam.

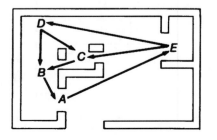

	A	B	C	D	E
Ax					
Rat					
Flea					
Jam					
Gum					

Tool 13 Using a Grid

Preparation: Copy pages 57 and 58 for students. Make page 56 an overhead.

Anticipatory Set: Show the students the grid on the overhead. Ask them to choose a location on the grid. Ask them how they would tell you where it is located. Lead the students to suggest how to locate a point on a grid.

Purpose: Explain that a grid is a set of horizontal and vertical lines. Where the lines meet is a point. Explain that the students are going to use the grid to solve problems.

Input: Define the *grid* as a set of horizontal and vertical lines. Explain that the place at which two lines meet is a *point*. Show how to find a point on the grid and how to go about labeling it. Explain that the number along the bottom always goes first, and the number on the side goes next. These two numbers are called a *number pair*.

Modeling: Choose one letter, and show how you use the bottom number and the side number to follow the lines to where they meet. Then, show how to write the number pair. Work on problems 1–12 with the class. Have volunteers touch the screen and trace the lines to find the point.

Guided Practice: Explain the directions of practice page 57. Review that the number along the bottom goes first in the number pair. Divide the class into partners. Have them work the problems and discuss how they got their answers.

Check for Understanding: Review the problems with the groups. Ask for volunteers to explain.

Independent Practice: Review the steps to use a grid. Pass out page 58. Read the directions, and go over the two processes of plotting the points and then using them to spell words. Monitor the students as they work independently.

Closure: Ask the students to review the parts of a grid. Ask them to explain their purpose. Then, have the students brainstorm different uses for grids in the real world.

Which Way Do I Go?

Some grids may have 4 sections. There will be negative numbers naming intersecting lines. Always start at 0. If the first coordinate is negative, move left to that number. If the second coordinate is negative, move down to that number.

Directions

Use the graph to find the coordinate for each location.

1. bank _____   **2.** police station _____

3. city hall _____   **4.** school _____

5. dry cleaner _____   **6.** clubhouse _____

7. Locate each point on the map by following the given directions. Label the point with the letter. Then write the coordinate.

A. Go 3 blocks east and then 4 blocks north.

_____

B. Go 5 blocks east and then 0 blocks north.

_____

C. Go 1 block east and then 1 block south.

_____

D. Go 1 block west and then 2 blocks north.

_____

E. Go 5 blocks west and then 1 block south.

_____

F. Go 4 blocks east and then 4 blocks south.

_____

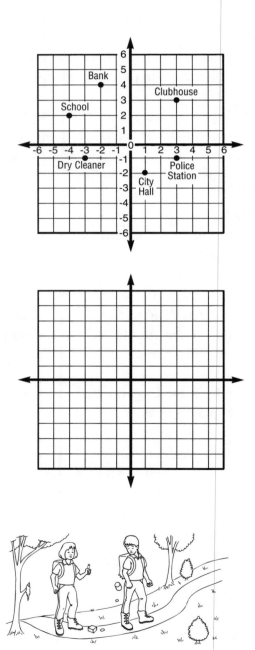

Unit 2: Math
Lesson Plans Using Graphic Organizers 6, SV 2074-5

Name _____ Date _____

The Point of Drawing

Coordinates can be used to draw pictures on a graph.
You do not need to write the letters on the graph—only the points.

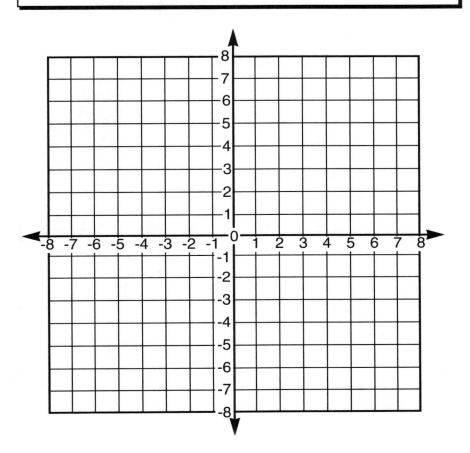

Directions

**Use the coordinates to make a picture on the graph. Mark each point in the order given.
Draw lines between the points with a ruler as you go.**

1. (1,5)   **2.** (1,2)   **3.** (2,2)   **4.** (2,-2)   **5.** (3,-2)

6. (3,-6)   **7.** (-3,-6)   **8.** (-3,-2)   **9.** (-2,-2)   **10.** (-2,2)

11. (-1,2)   **12.** (-1,5)   **13.** (1,5)

Unit 2: Math

Riddled with Letters

Check the numbers in each pair carefully. Remember that if the first number is negative, you move left. If the second number is negative, you move down.

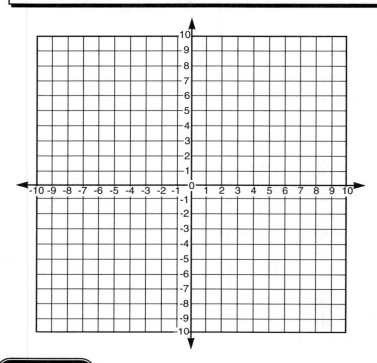

Directions

Use the number pairs to mark the points on the grid.

1. (5,5) = A   **2.** (1,10) = B   **3.** (-3,3) = C   **4.** (10,6) = D

5. (5,2) = E   **6.** (-7,-5) = F   **7.** (7,-9) = G   **8.** (-5,-1) = H

9. (8,4) = I   **10.** (2,4) = J   **11.** (9,-4) = K   **12.** (10,1) = L

13. (6,-1) = M   **14.** (8,-7) = N   **15.** (-2,3) = O   **16.** (-2,-6) = P

17. (-9,8) = Q   **18.** (4,0) = R   **19.** (-5,7) = S   **20.** (-4,-7) = T

21. (0,7) = U   **22.** (2,-9) = V   **23.** (-10,-8) = W   **24.** (-1,1) = X

25. (-4,-4) = Y   **26.** (8,10) = Z

Use each coordinate below to decode the riddle.

Why did the computer go to work out at the gym?

___ ___ ___ ___ ___   ___ ___   ___ ___ ___ ___
(8,4) (-4,-7) (-5,-1) (5,5) (10,6) (-4,-7) (-2,3) (-10,-8) (-2,3) (4,0) (9,-4)

___ ___ ___   ___ ___ ___   ___ ___ ___ ___ ___ ___ .
(-2,3) (-7,-5) (-7,-5) (8,4) (-4,-7) (-5,7) (-7,-5) (10,1) (-2,3) (-2,-6) (-2,-6) (-4,-4)

Tool 14 Finding the Frequency

Preparation: Copy pages 61 and 62 for students. Make page 60 an overhead. Each set of partners will need a die.

Anticipatory Set: Ask the students to predict the number of students in the class with brown eyes. Remind them to think of the total number of students and the number of those who might have brown eyes. After they calculate the information, have the students write the information as a ratio (brown eyes/all colored eyes).

Purpose: Explain that the students are finding the probability of students with brown eyes. They will be finding the probability by finding the frequency.

Input: Define *frequency* as the number of times an event happens. *Relative frequency* is another word for *probability*. The probability is the ratio of the probable events to the total number of outcomes.

Modeling: Place page 60 on the overhead. Read the information out loud. Review the definition of *frequency*. Then, work the problems using the ratio between the color of backpacks and the total number of backpacks.

Guided Practice: Review the definitions of *frequency* and *probability*. Pass out page 61. Divide the class into partners. Pass out a number cube. Have the students roll it 25 times. They will record their data in the chart. Then, they will use this information to find the frequency of several numbers.

Check for Understanding: Review the process of finding the probability. Then, read the problems, and answer them out loud. Have different partners volunteer to solve the problems. Have the students explain the steps they took to derive that answer.

Independent Practice: Pass out page 62. Have the students work the relative frequency problems. Remind them to use the information in the chart and the sample problem.

Closure: Review the definitions of *frequency*, *relative frequency*, and *probability*. Then, have the students think of other things of which they might need to find the frequency.

Name _____ Date _____

Backpack Facts

> Probability is sometimes called *relative frequency*. A table makes it easier to show the ratio of the probable events to the total number of outcomes.

Lucy did a survey of her class. She asked her classmates what color backpack they had. She recorded the results on a table.

Backpack Colors

Color	Number of Students
Blue	8
Red	5
Black	4
Green	7
Gray	6

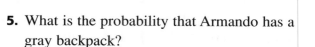

Use the table to answer the questions below.

1. What are the possible outcomes?

   _____

2. What color of backpacks is the most popular?

   _____

3. What color of backpack is the least popular?

   _____

4. What is the probability that Karen has a red backpack?

   _____

5. What is the probability that Armando has a gray backpack?

   _____

6. What is the probability that Larry does not have a blue backpack?

   _____

7. What is the probability that Danielle has a red or green backpack?

   _____

8. What is the probability that Nolan or Anita has a gray backpack?

   _____

Name _____ Date _____

Rolling Along

Number shapes, like cubes, are often used when playing games. You can use your probability skills to predict what you will roll.

If you roll a number cube 25 times, how many times do you think each number will show? Make a guess. Then get a number cube and roll it 25 times. Record your information on the table.

Number Cube Probability

Number	Guess	Tally	Relative Frequency	Frequency
1				
2				
3				
4				
5				
6				

Directions

Answer the questions below.

1. Was your guess correct? Why or why not?

_____

2. Based on your frequency chart, what would you predict your chances are of rolling each number if you toss the dice 100 times?

1 _____   2 _____   3 _____

4 _____   5 _____   6 _____

© Steck-Vaughn Company

Unit 2: Math

Lesson Plans Using Graphic Organizers 6, SV 2074-5

Pets with Proportion

You can use relative frequencies to make predictions about larger groups.

Hector asked 50 of his classmates how many pets they owned. He made a table to show his data. On the table, he included a column to show frequency outcomes.

To predict how many out of 100 students own 3 pets, he wrote a formula, called a proportion, and solved it.

$$\frac{n}{100} = \frac{6}{50}$$

$n \times 50 = 6 \times 100 \qquad n \times 50 = 600 \qquad n = 12$

Pets Owned

Event	Relative Frequency	Frequency
0 pets	5	$\frac{1}{10}$
1 pet	18	$\frac{9}{25}$
2 pets	20	$\frac{2}{5}$
3 pets	6	$\frac{3}{25}$
4 pets	1	$\frac{1}{50}$
Total	50	1

Directions

Answer the questions below.

1. How many out of 100 students own 2 pets?

   _____

2. How many out of 200 students own 3 pets?

   _____

3. How many out of 200 students own 2 pets?

   _____

4. How many out of 100 students own 2 or 3 pets?

   _____

5. How many out of 200 students own 1 pet?

   _____

6. How many out of 100 students own fewer than 4 pets?

   _____

7. How many out of 500 students own 1 pet?

   _____

8. How many out of 1,000 students own 3 pets?

   _____

Tool 15   Calculating the Cost of Energy

Preparation: Make copies of pages 65 and 66. Make an overhead of page 64.

Anticipatory Set: Ask the students to define *energy*. Ask them to think about what it is, how it is used, and how we get it. Have the students brainstorm a list of different types of energy and how they are used. Then circle *electricity*, and explain that that is the energy they will observe in this lesson.

Purpose: Explain that electricity is a form of energy. In the United States, $\frac{1}{5}$ of our energy is used in the home.

Input: Define *energy* as the ability to move things. Then define *electricity* as the energy that flows though wires. Power plants that produce electricity often use a variety of energy sources, such as water or fuels.

Modeling: Place page 64 on the overhead. Read the information about electricity and energy out loud. Ask the students if they can think of the different appliances in their own homes that use electricity. Then, use the table to calculate the cost of one year for each appliance. Discuss why it is important to maintain appliances in good working condition and to buy energy-saving products. Ask how the appliance's condition relates to its cost of use for one year.

Guided Practice: Divide the class into partners. Explain that they are going to be energy-conscious consumers. They are going to figure out the cost of running a refrigerator based on its sales tag. Pass out page 65, and have the students complete it with their partners.

Check for Understanding: Review the definition of *energy* and *electricity*. Then, ask for several volunteers to read their answers for problems 1 through 3. Discuss each answer, and have the students explain how they derived their answers. After reviewing the three problems, ask the students if this would be a good, energy-saving appliance.

Independent Practice: Explain that the students are going to continue to examine the cost of electricity. They are going to review information from a chart and graph it on a bar graph. The students will work independently. Pass out page 66, and read the directions to make sure the students understand the instructions.

Closure: Ask the students to think about why they should conserve energy. Then, have them give examples of ways they can reduce the amount of energy they use at home or at school.

The Cost of Energy

About $\frac{1}{5}$ of the energy we use in the United States is used in our homes. To help conserve energy, we should become aware of the cost of using appliances and buy appliances that use less energy.

The chart below shows how much electricity is consumed by different appliances in a year. Electricity used is measured in units called kilowatt-hours. If you know how much you are charged for each kilowatt-hour you use, you can determine what it costs to run each appliance. Let's say it cost 7 cents ($0.07) for each kilowatt-hour. What does it cost to run each appliance on the table? The first one is done for you.

Directions

Fill in the table.

Energy Use

Appliances	Energy (KWH) Used in One Year	Cost for One Year
1. Air conditioner	450	$0.07/KWH = $31.50
2. Clothes dryer	900	
3. Lighting system	1,000	
4. Range	1,200	
5. Refrigerator	1,125	
6. Television	200	

Name _____ Date _____

Is It Cost Effective?

Certain appliances are labeled with tags that show what it costs to use them for a year. Look at the sample Energy Cost Label from a refrigerator on the next page. It tells you that it costs $91 to run the refrigerator for a year when a kilowatt-hour costs about 5 cents. It compares the cost of using this refrigerator to other refrigerators. It also gives yearly costs when a kilowatt-hour costs more or less than 5 cents.

Directions

Study the label below. Then answer the questions.

1. What is the yearly cost if a kilowatt-hour costs 10 cents?

_____

2. What is the cost to run the model with the lowest energy costs?

_____

3. Energy costs 5 cents a kilowatt-hour. How many kilowatt-hours are used in a year by a refrigerator costing $90 a year to run?

_____

Refrigerator-Freezer
Capacity: 23 Cubic Feet

(Name of Corporation)
Model(s) AH503, AH504, AH507
Type of Defrost: Full Automatic

ENERGYGUIDE

Estimates on the scale are based on a national average electric rate of 4.97¢ per kilowatt hour

Only models with 22.5 to 24.4 cubic feet are compared in the scale

Model with lowest energy cost

$91

Model with highest energy cost

$68
▼

THIS ▼ MODEL
Estimated yearly energy cost

$132
▼

Your cost will vary depending on your local energy rate and how you use the product. This energy cost is based on U.S. Government standard tests.

How much will this model cost you to run yearly?

		Yearly cost
		Estimated yearly $ cost shown below.
Cost per kilowatt hour	2¢	$36
	4¢	$73
	6¢	$109
	8¢	$146
	10¢	$182
	12¢	$218

Ask your salesperson or local utility for the energy rate (cost per kilowatt hour) in your area.

Important Removal of this label before consumer purchase is a violation of federal law (42 U.S.C. 6302)

(Part No. 3710261)

Name _____ Date _____

Graphing Electricity Costs

How much energy do appliances use? To find out, look at the chart. Appliances are given wattage ratings. Appliances with higher wattage numbers use more electric power than ones with lower wattage numbers. Compare the cost of running various appliances for one hour.

Appliances	Typical Wattage	Estimated Cost Per Hour
Radio	75	1¢
Color TV	300	3¢
Vacuum cleaner	650	7¢
Hand-held hair dryer	600	6¢
Clothes dryer	5,000	50¢
Electric broiler	3,600	36¢
Dishwasher	1,200	12¢
CD player	100	1¢

Directions

Complete the bar graph using data from the chart. The first appliance, a radio, is done for you.

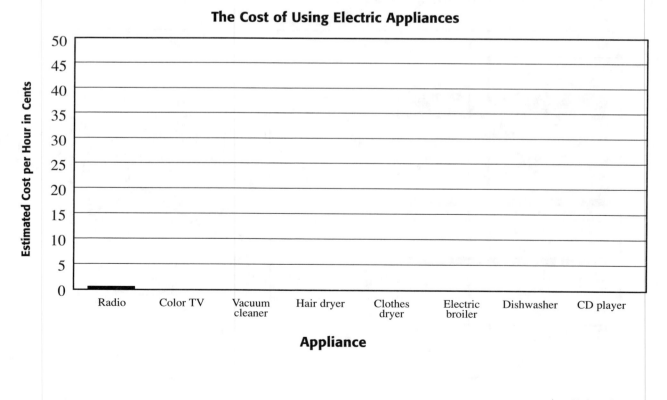

The Cost of Using Electric Appliances

 **Using the Scientific Method: Acids and Bases**

Preparation: Gather pink and blue litmus paper, dish soap, carbonated drinks, permanent markers, lemon juice, sugar water, small paper cups, and milk for each pair of partners. You can set up a cup with the liquid in it at stations, or have enough for each set of partners. Copy pages 69 and 70 for each student. Make an overhead of page 68.

Anticipatory Set: Write the words *acid* and *base* on the board. Ask the students if they can define these words or give examples of either word.

Purpose: Explain that the students will use the scientific method to discover if certain liquids are acids or bases using litmus paper to test their predictions.

Input: Define *acid* as a compound that tastes sour, and *base* as a compound that tastes bitter. Explain that some compounds are neither acids nor bases, but are neutral.

Modeling: Each student should have page 69 and page 70. Place page 68 on the overhead. Read through the information and the directions together. Explain how you want the students to do the experiment—whether they move to stations or if they will have an entire set of compounds for each set of partners.

Guided Practice: Have the students complete the first part of their scientific method sheet. Have them explain what they are going to do, or state the problem. Then, have the students make predictions about what will be an acid and what will be a base. Then, have them write a hypothesis, or a guess about their results.

Check for Understanding: Review what the students wrote. Then, have them perform the experiments. Remind them to complete their charts with their results.

Independent Practice: After the students have completed the experiments, they need to complete the scientific method sheet by answering the questions.

Closure: Review the definitions of *acid* and *base*. Then, have several students compare their results. Ask them how this information can be useful to the students.

Name _____ Date _____

Acids and Bases

Compounds can be divided into two groups—acids and bases. There are many kinds of acids and bases in your home and school. Acids tastes sour. Lemon juice is an example of an acid. Bases taste bitter. Baking soda is an example of a base. Chemicals can be acids and bases, too. Sulfuric acid is used in car batteries. Bleach, a base, is used to whiten clothes. Some substances are neither acids nor bases. They are neutral. (Caution: Never taste an unknown substance.)

Litmus paper is a way to test a substance chemically to discover which compound it is. Litmus paper comes in colors of blue and pink. A substance that is a base will change pink litmus to blue. A substance that is an acid will change blue litmus to pink. If both strips stay the same color, then the substance is neutral. It is neither a base nor an acid.

You will need:	
pink and blue litmus paper	lemon juice
dish soap	sugar water
carbonated drink	small paper cups
permanent maker	milk

Directions

1. Label each cup with the name of the substance. Pour a small amount of each into the cup.

2. Complete the hypothesis and prediction.

3. Dip a strip of blue litmus into the first substance. Did it change color? Record your findings on the table on your page.

4. Dip a strip of pink litmus into the same cup. Did it change color? Record your findings on the table on your page.

5. Record whether each substance is a base, an acid, or neutral in the last column of the table.

Name _____   Date _____

Scientific Method: Acid, Base, or Neutral?

Directions

Answer the questions and complete the charts.

1. **Problem:** Identify a problem or question you want to investigate.

   _____

   _____

2. **Hypothesis:** Tell what you think the results will be of your experiment.

   _____

   _____

3. **Prediction:** Is the compound an acid, a base, or neutral?

Material:	Is it an Acid, a Base, or Neutral?
Lemon Juice	
Milk	
Dish Soap	
Sugar Water	
Carbonated Drink	

Go on to the next page.

Name _____ Date _____

Scientific Method: Acid, Base, or Neutral, p. 2

Directions

Fill in the table. Then answer the questions.

4.   **Testing Household Substances**

Material:	Reaction to blue litmus paper	Reaction to pink litmus paper	Is it an Acid, a Base, or Neutral?
Lemon Juice			
Milk			
Dish Soap			
Sugar Water			
Carbonated Drink			

5. Which substances turned the litmus paper pink?

_____

6. Which substance turned the litmus paper blue?

_____

7. Which substances are acids? Explain.

_____

_____

8. Which substance is a base? Explain.

_____

_____

9. Which substances are neutral? Explain.

_____

_____

(Tool 17) Exploring Biomes

Preparation: Copy pages 73 and 74 for each student. Make an overhead of page 72.

Anticipatory Set: Write the word *desert* on the board. Have the students describe characteristics of a desert. After they have given several descriptors, tell them that they are describing a biome.

Purpose: Explain that the students are going to look at the six different biomes of the Earth and some of their major characteristics. Then, explain that they will explore in more detail the biome of the rain forest.

Input: Define *biome* as a large community of plants and animals that is determined by the climate.

Modeling: Place page 72 on the overhead. Read through the information provided on the top of the page. Discuss with the students the differences between the six biomes. Then, complete the chart on the bottom of the page together, and answer the questions.

Guided Practice: Divide the class into partners. Pass out page 73. Have them read the passage about the tropical rain forest. The students will read the passage and highlight important information, then discuss the information on the graph.

Check for Understanding: Ask the students to share some of the information they learned about the rain forest. Then, ask them questions about the graph.

Independent Practice: Pass out page 74. Read the directions, and explain that the students will use the information from the passage and the graph to answer the questions.

Closure: Review the definition of *biome*. Ask the students to give examples of the six biomes. Then, ask them to state characteristics of the tropical rain forest. Have students discuss how the Earth would be affected if the tropical rain forest biome disappeared.

Name _____ Date _____

Biomes

A **biome** is a large community of plants and animals. The type of biome is determined by the climate and the kinds of plants found there. There are six major land biomes in the world.

Tropical rain forests grow where the climate is warm and rainy. Most of the animal life is found in the trees. Rain forests are important because they produce oxygen, which supports life.

Deciduous forests have warm or hot summers and cold winters. Deciduous trees lose their leaves every fall. Deer, squirrels, foxes, owls, and snakes are found in deciduous forests.

Boreal forests grow in places with very cold, snowy winters and short growing seasons. The trees are mostly evergreens. In this type of forest, you will find deer, bears, snowshoe hares, and beavers.

On the **arctic tundra**, the winters are long and cold, and the summers are short and cool. Animals on the tundra, such as the snowy owl, are adapted for cold weather. They also blend in with the snow.

Grasslands have winters that are cold and snowy and summers that are hot and dry. Many small animals, such as ground squirrels, prairie dogs, and many kinds of birds, are found in the grasslands.

Because **deserts** receive very little rainfall, the plants there are far apart so they don't compete with each other for moisture. The desert supports many animals, such as mice, snakes, and coyotes.

Directions

Complete the chart by using words from the article. Then answer the questions.

Biome	Description
	1. long, cold winters; animals blend with snow
	2. warm summers, cold winters; trees lose leaves
	3. receive little rainfall; plants are far apart
	4. cold, snowy winters; evergreen trees
	5. hot, dry summers; home to prairie dogs
	6. warm and rainy; produce much oxygen

7. A biome is _____

_____ .

8. Name the biome where you live. _____

Unit 3: Science

Name _____ Date _____

Tropical Rain Forests

The tropical rain forest is home to more species of plants and animals than all the world's other land biomes combined. Some types of organisms can exist only in the tropical rain forest. Unfortunately, destruction of the tropical rain forest is occurring at an alarming rate. Of an original 16 million square kilometers (6 million square miles) of tropical rain forest, only about half remains. Some parts have been cleared to provide land for farming or for grazing cattle. Some parts have been destroyed as the hardwoods they contain are harvested. Plans exist for hydroelectric dams that would flood thousands of additional square kilometers of the rain forest. Current information suggests that destruction of the forest may be as high as 120,000 square kilometers (46,000 square miles) annually. In Brazil alone, as much as 80,000 square kilometers (31,000 square miles) of rain forest is destroyed annually, although this rate may have decreased recently. It is difficult to estimate the amount of forest being lost. In addition to field studies, aerial photographs and satellite photos have been used.

This circle graph shows the amount of tropical rain forest that is cleared every year in nine countries.

Tropical Rain Forest Cleared
(hectares)

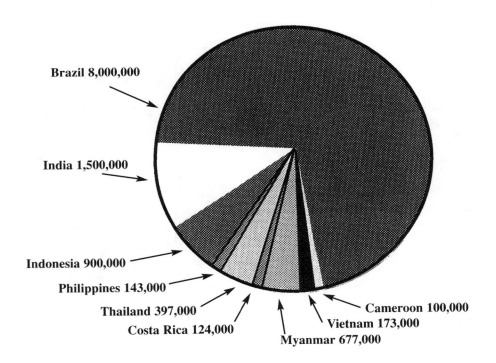

Brazil 8,000,000
India 1,500,000
Indonesia 900,000
Philippines 143,000
Thailand 397,000
Costa Rica 124,000
Cameroon 100,000
Vietnam 173,000
Myanmar 677,000

Go on to the next page.

Tropical Rain Forests, p. 2

Directions

Answer the questions below.

1. According to the circle graph, which country loses the most rain forest each year?

   _____

2. How much of a loss does Costa Rica have compared with Brazil?

   _____

   _____

3. What is the total amount of tropical rain forest land that is destroyed each year in all nine countries?

   _____

   _____

4. Why do you think people are concerned about tropical rain forests being destroyed?

   _____

   _____

   _____

5. What kinds of things can people do to stop tropical rain forests from being destroyed?

   _____

   _____

   _____

   _____

   _____

   _____

Tool 18 Determining Traits

Preparation: Copy pages 77 and 78 for each student. Make an overhead of page 76.

Anticipatory Set: Ask the students to think of one trait that they share with at least one member of their family, such as the same color hair, eyes, nose shape, etc. Then, ask them to think about a trait that they alone have in their family.

Purpose: Explain that these traits come from recessive and dominant genes that are passed from generation to generation. Tell the students that they are going to make some observations and predictions about their own traits.

Input: Explain that genes determine the traits of all living things; they come in pairs, but may not be identical; and offspring from two parents inherit one gene from each of their parents' gene pair. Define *dominant genes* as the stronger genes, and the weaker genes are called *recessive genes*.

Modeling: Place page 76 on the overhead. Read through the information about Mendel. Discuss dominant and recessive traits. Then, work through the problems about the plants, and discuss your reasoning on how you determined the offspring.

Guided Practice: Pass out page 77. Explain that the students will now apply Mendel's theory of dominant and recessive traits to their classmates. Divide the class into groups of four. Explain that they are going to take a survey of their entire class. They are going to find out how many students have dominant and recessive traits. Then, they will answer the two questions.

Check for Understanding: Refocus the students. Have several students share the information their group discovered. Ask them how many students have dominant traits for hair, dimples, and light eyes, then ask about the recessive traits. Ask them to discuss what their information tells them about their classmates.

Independent Practice: Pass out page 78. Tell the students that they are now going to determine if they have more dominant or recessive traits. They will complete a chart about themselves. Then, they will determine if they have dominant or recessive traits.

Closure: Review what genes are and how they determine the traits living things inherit. Ask the students how this information is useful to them.

Name _____ Date _____

A Monk Called Mendel

Gregor Mendel is known as the Father of Genetics. Because of his work, scientists know that there are two heredity factors for every trait, one of which comes from each parent. They also know that of these genes, some are dominant and some are recessive.

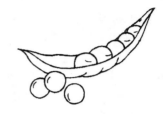

Dominant Traits	Recessive Traits
tall	short
round seeds	wrinkled seeds
yellow seeds	green seeds
flowers along entire stem	flowers at top of stem

The table above shows dominant and recessive traits in pea plants. Use this table to predict traits that would appear in each of the pea-plant crosses described below. Write your answers in the "Offspring" squares.

1. Plant 1   ×   **Plant 2**   =   **Offspring**

tall wrinkled seeds, yellow seeds, flowers along entire stem

tall round seeds, yellow seeds, flowers at top of stem

2. Plant 1   ×   **Plant 2**   =   **Offspring**

short yellow seeds, round seeds, flowers along entire stem

tall green seeds, wrinkled seeds, flowers along entire stem

3. Plant 1   ×   **Plant 2**   =   **Offspring**

tall round seeds, yellow seeds, flowers along entire stem

short wrinkled seeds, green seeds, flowers at top of stem

Unit 3: Science

Lesson Plans Using Graphic Organizers 6, SV 2074-5

Name _____ Date _____

Dominant and Recessive Traits

Directions

Do This

List how many of your classmates appear to have dominant or recessive traits for curly hair or straight hair, dimples or no dimples, and light eyes or dark eyes.

Keep a Record

Use your data to complete this chart.
(Don't forget to include yourself in the count.)

Dominant Traits	Number	Recessive Traits	Number
Curly Hair		Straight Hair	
Dimples		No Dimples	
Light Eyes		Dark Eyes	

Answer the questions below.

1. Do more students in your class have dominant or recessive traits?

   _____

2. Why do you think this is the case?

   _____

   _____

Name _____ Date _____

Dominant or Recessive?

   You can find out about some traits you have inherited. You can also find out something about what genes you have. If you show a dominant trait, you have at least one dominant gene. If you show a recessive trait, you have two recessive genes.

Directions

1. Fill in the chart with the traits that you have. You may need a mirror to help you.

Trait	Your Trait	How Inherited
Hair  curly 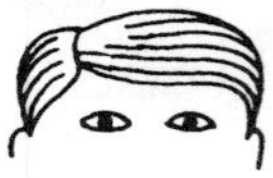 straight		dominant recessive
Earlobes  detached  attached		dominant recessive
Tongue  roller  nonroller		dominant recessive
Cheek  dimples 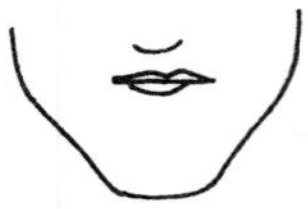 smooth		dominant recessive
Chin 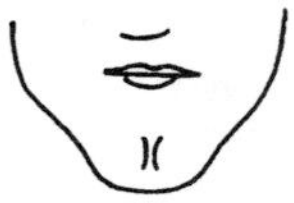 cleft  smooth		dominant recessive

2. Determine as much as you can about your genes. Circle *dominant* if you have inherited a dominant trait. Circle *recessive* if you have inherited a recessive trait.

Unit 3: Science
Lesson Plans Using Graphic Organizers 6, SV 2074-5

Tool 19 Food Chains

Preparation: Copy pages 81 and 82 for each student. Make an overhead of page 80.

Anticipatory Set: Ask the students to think of things that happen in a cycle. Then have them think about food chains. Ask what it means to be in a food chain.

Purpose: Explain that the students are going to observe different examples of food chains and their components.

Input: Define a *food chain* as a process in which all living things are a part. Tell them that every food chain begins with a producer and ends with a decomposer.

Modeling: Place page 80 on the overhead. Read through the information at the top of the page. Discuss the differences between the producers, decomposers, and consumers. Then, observe the prairie food chain. Discuss the chain of consumers. Answer the questions together with the students.

Guided Practice: Pass out page 81. Divide the class into partners. Explain that they are going to look at another food chain and discuss its components. The students will work with their partners. Review the definition of *producer*, *consumer*, and *decomposer*.

Check for Understanding: Ask several sets of partners to share the answers they found for the five questions. Discuss the food chain and how the parts interrelate.

Independent Practice: Pass out page 82. Explain that the students have observed two examples of food chains. Now they are going to look at a food web in which several food chains intertwine in an environment. They will study the food web and use the information they find to answer the questions.

Closure: Review what a food chain is and its purpose in a given environment. Ask the students to think of other examples of food chains. Then, ask them to think about a food chain in which they are the consumers.

Name _____ Date _____

A Prairie Food Chain

All living things are part of a food chain. Every food chain begins with *producers* (green plants) and ends with *decomposers* (bacteria and fungi). The organisms that feed on producers are called *first-order consumers*. Those that feed on first-order consumers are *second-order consumers*.

The picture shows two food chains in a prairie community. Food chains are made up of producers, consumers, and decomposers. Two or more food chains can be linked together by a common producer. Study the picture and then complete the statements below.

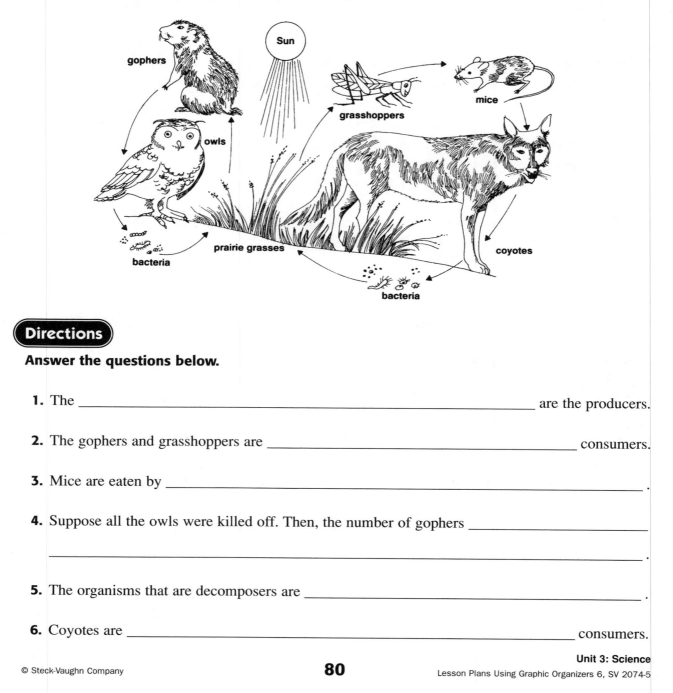

Directions

Answer the questions below.

1. The _____ are the producers.

2. The gophers and grasshoppers are _____ consumers.

3. Mice are eaten by _____ .

4. Suppose all the owls were killed off. Then, the number of gophers _____

_____ .

5. The organisms that are decomposers are _____ .

6. Coyotes are _____ consumers.

Name _____ Date _____

An Ocean Food Chain

A food chain shows how animals depend on other organisms for food. Most ocean food chains begin with plant plankton.

There are two types of plankton—animal and plant. Plant plankton captures light energy from the Sun and converts it to food. Most of the animals in the sea, including animal plankton, depend on plant plankton for food. All these tiny plants use only a half percent of the light energy that strikes the surface of the ocean. Yet they help feed an ocean full of animals.

Study the following food chain.

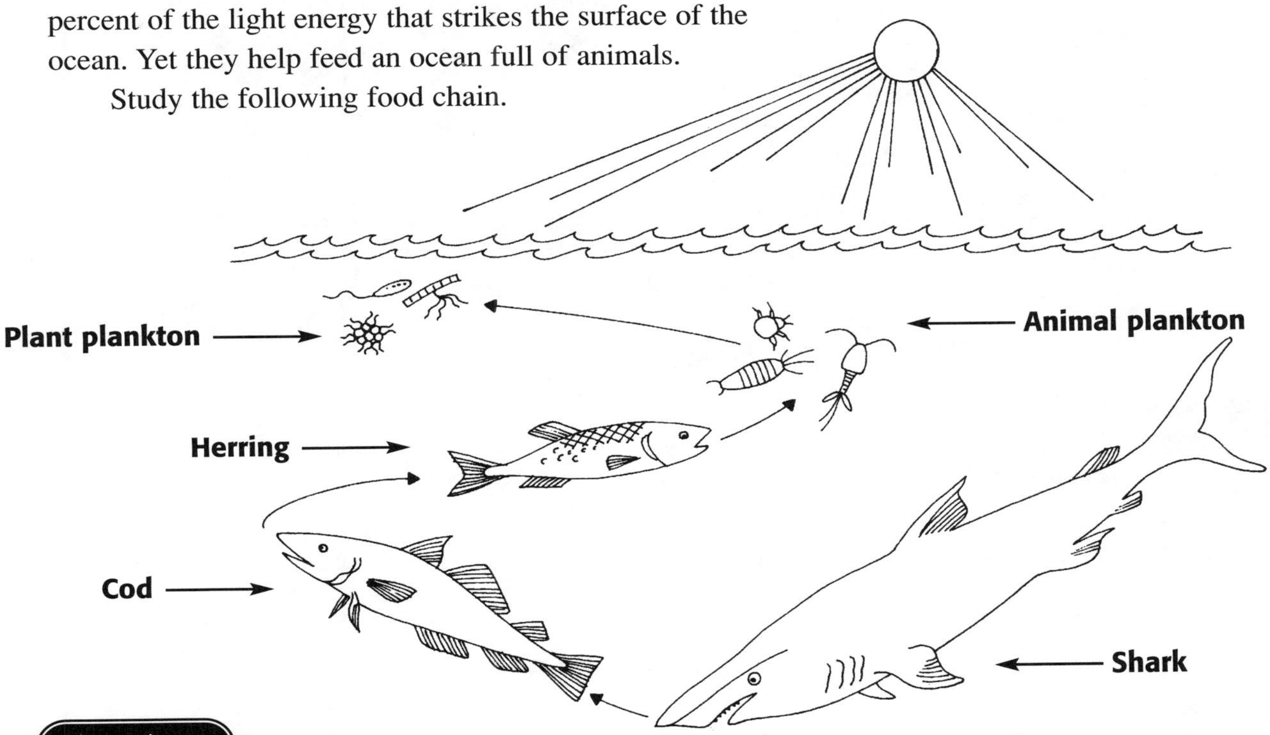

Directions

Answer the questions below.

1. What does the cod eat? _____

2. What eats the cod? _____

3. Where does the energy for this food chain come from? _____

4. What is the smallest organism in this food chain? _____

5. What would happen if all plant plankton suddenly disappeared?

_____

_____

Name _____ Date _____

A Food Web

A food chain shows how animals depend on other organisms for food. A food web shows all the possible food chains in an environment. Study the drawing below. It shows a food web in a field and meadow.

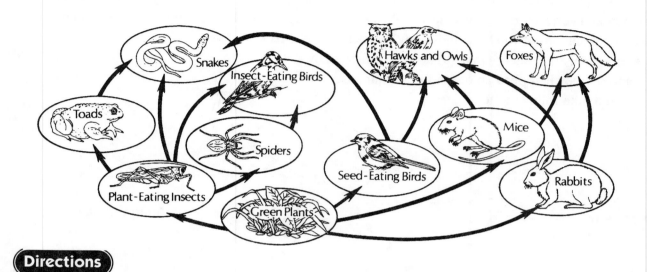

Directions

Answer the questions below.

1. Name at least five relationships shown in the food web.

_____
_____
_____
_____
_____

2. If there were no foxes, what would probably happen to the number of rabbits in the area?

_____
_____
_____

3. If more seed-eating birds come into the meadow, would the snakes be affected? _____
Explain your answer. _____

_____
_____

Tool 20 Reading Maps

Preparation: Copy pages 85 and 86 for students. Make page 84 an overhead.

Anticipatory Set: Have the students brainstorm different reasons they use maps. List them on the board.

Purpose: Explain that the students will read various maps to find information that specific maps provide.

Input: Explain that some maps provide information about population, precipitation, and elevation. These are maps that provide specific details.

Modeling: Place page 84 on the overhead. Examine the information provided in the title and the map key. Ask several students what information is provided in the key. Then, answer the questions using the map.

Guided Practice: Divide the class into partners. Pass out page 85. Explain that they are going to look at another type of map that shows population. Read the directions and review the map key with the students. Have them work through the questions with their partners.

Check for Understanding: Review the information provided in this map. Then, go over the answers to the questions. Call on several students to share their answers.

Independent Practice: Pass out the map for independent practice, page 86. Explain the directions. Tell the students that this map shows elevation. Define *elevation* as the height above sea level. Tell the students to use the map to answer the questions.

Closure: Review the parts of a map. Have students brainstorm different types of maps they may use and instances in which they would use them.

Name _____ Date _____

Precipitation Map

Directions

Study the map. Then answer the questions.

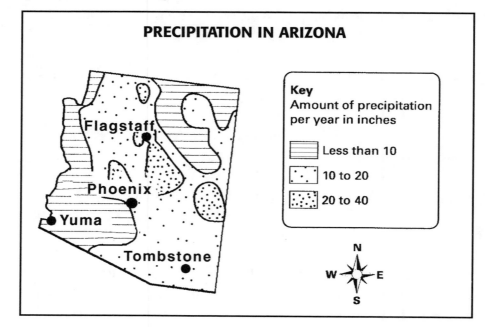

1. About how much precipitation does Phoenix receive each year?

_____

2. Which city receives less than 10 inches per year?

_____

3. Of the cities shown on the map, which receives the most precipitation each year?

_____

4. Which town might be in a desert? Explain.

_____

_____

_____

Name _____ Date _____

Population Map

Directions

Look at the map. Then answer the questions.

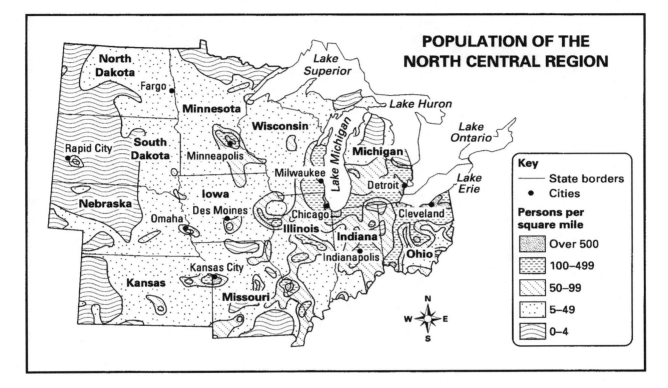

POPULATION OF THE
NORTH CENTRAL REGION

Key
— State borders
• Cities
Persons per square mile
Over 500
100–499
50–99
5–49
0–4

1. What is the name of this map?

_____

2. What symbol is used to show cities?

_____

3. Which state is directly south of Minnesota?

_____

4. About how many people per square mile live in Fargo, North Dakota?

_____

© Steck-Vaughn Company

Lesson Plans Using Graphic Organizers 6, SV 2074-5

Name _____ Date _____

Elevation Map

Directions

Study the map. Then answer the questions.

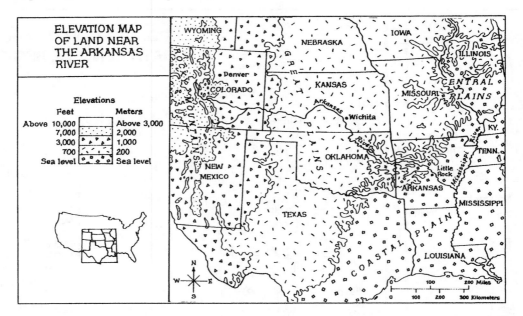

ELEVATION MAP
OF LAND NEAR
THE ARKANSAS
RIVER

Elevations

Feet		Meters
Above 10,000		Above 3,000
7,000		2,000
3,000		1,000
700		200
Sea level		Sea level

1. Where is the Arkansas River's source? What is the elevation?

_____

2. Where does the mouth of the Arkansas River end? What is the elevation?

_____

3. What states does the Arkansas River flow through?

_____

4. How many feet does the Arkansas River drop in elevation from its source to its mouth?

_____

Tool 21 Using a KWL Chart

Preparation: Copy pages 88, 89, and 90 for students. Make an overhead of page 88.

Anticipatory Set: Show the students the overhead of page 88. Have the students observe the *KWL* chart. Have them predict what the *K, W,* and *L* stand for. Then, explain that they will use this chart to help them understand a new concept.

Purpose: Explain that the *KWL* chart will help students organize what they know, create a purpose for reading, and discover the answers to their own questions.

Input: Explain that the *K* in the chart stands for "*Know,*" the *W* stands for "*Want to Know,*" and the *L* stands for "*Learned.*"

Modeling: Pass out a copy of the *KWL* chart on page 88 to students. Identify the topic, *Incas.* Model how the students will complete a *KWL* chart. Start with *K:* ask what the students know about Incas. Have them write in a few things as you write in their responses on the overhead. Then, explain that in the *W* column, the students will write at least five questions they would like to find out about the Incas. The students will write five questions in the column. Call on several students to read their questions out loud.

Guided Practice: Pass out page 89. Explain that they will now read the passage with a partner. While they read, have them underline any information that they did not know about the Incas or information that would answer their questions.

Check for Understanding: Ask the students to state some of the things they now know about the Incas. Have several partners share their information.

Independent Practice: Using the information the students found about the Incas, have the students complete the *L* column. Explain that they will write at least five things that they learned about the Incas in the *L* column.

Closure: Have students review the purpose of the *KWL* chart. Ask them what the *K, W,* and *L* stand for. Then, ask the students to tell what they learned about the Incas. Have them give examples of how they can apply this *KWL* chart to other things they do in school or at home.

Name _____ Date _____

KWL Chart

Topic: _____

K	W	L

Unit 4: Social Studies

Lesson Plans Using Graphic Organizers 6, SV 2074-5

Name _____ Date _____

The Lost City of the Incas

"If you're looking for Inca ruins, I might be able to help you," said Arteaga.

Hiram Bingham, an American explorer, looked closely at the Indian farmer. Bingham and his group were exploring South America for Inca ruins. They had spent many days wandering through the jungles of Peru, and now they were camped on the banks of the Urubamba River. It seemed unlikely that this farmer could lead them to anything important.

Most of the group stayed in camp. But Bingham wanted to follow every lead, so the two men set off into the jungle.

Arteaga led Bingham up a mountain. It was a rainy July morning in 1911. For four hours the men chopped their way through trees, vines, and jungle plants. The climb was steep, and sometimes they had to crawl on their hands and knees. They climbed higher and higher. Bingham grew tired and began to have doubts that they would find any ruins. But as they came around a hill, he saw something that was very surprising.

About a hundred stone terraces stretched out in front of them. As they walked on, they found the ruins of well-built houses and a cave lined with stone. Above the cave was a temple made of pure white granite. Bingham later wrote, "It took my breath away. What could this place be?"

What Bingham saw was Machu Picchu (MA choo PEEK choo), one of the greatest ruins in South America. The Indians who lived nearby knew about it, but for 400 years it had been their secret. Bingham was the first explorer to discover the amazing Machu Picchu.

Machu Picchu was indeed a city that took one's breath away. Everywhere Bingham looked, surprise followed surprise. The Incas had built beautiful stone buildings. The stones in the white granite walls had been carefully cut and pieced together. Bingham said, "Clearly, it was the work of a master artist."

Go on to the next page.

The Lost City of the Incas, p. 2

The Incas had built the city on the top of a mountain. It was surrounded by jungles. Other mountains towered above it. Two thousand feet below, Bingham could see the winding Urubamba River. No wonder it had taken explorers so long to discover this place!

No one doubts that Machu Picchu was built by the Incas. The style of the buildings is like Inca buildings found in other locations. But how did they build it? How could they have built such a beautiful city in such a remote place? The Incas had no written language. They had not even discovered the wheel. They had no animals to carry big loads, yet somehow, they had moved stones weighing many tons. These stones were used to build huge walls. The Incas did not use mortar to hold the stones in place. They carved the stones so that they would fit together tightly.

How could the Incas have cut the stones so exactly? They had no iron tools that could have done the job. So how were the stones cut? No one knows the answer.

No one has lived in Machu Picchu for more than 500 years. What happened to the Incas who lived there? Were they all killed by disease? Were they attacked by an enemy?

Did someone commit a terrible crime? Inca law stated that if someone committed a very bad crime, the guilty person had to die. Sometimes friends, family, and neighbors were killed, too. In fact, a whole town might be killed. Is that what happened to the people of Machu Picchu?

We know that Inca tribes sometimes fought each other. When one tribe beat another tribe, often everyone was killed. Is that what happened to the people of Machu Picchu?

Scientists search for clues to solve the mysteries of Machu Picchu. Hidden by mountains and clouds, this empty city is a puzzle. Why did the Incas build it? How did they build it? Why did they disappear without a trace? Perhaps one day we'll find the answers to these questions.

Tool 22 Comparing and Contrasting

Preparation: Make copies of pages 93 and 94 for students. Make an overhead of pages 92 and 93. Bring a pair of dress shoes and a pair of running shoes.

Anticipatory Set: Show the two different types of shoes. Ask the students to describe how the shoes are similar. Then, have them describe how they are different.

Purpose: Explain that what the students are doing is comparing and contrasting. Tell them that comparing and contrasting help find the similarities that two things share and acknowledge their differences.

Input: Define *comparing* as finding the similarities of two things and *contrasting* as finding the differences of two things.

Modeling: Show the students the two passages of the different regions' resources on page 92 on the overhead. Read them out loud. As you read, comment on how things are the same for both the River and Lakes states and the West states regions. Then put the Venn diagram on the overhead. Explain how to set up the diagram with the two regions being in separate circles. Then, ask the students to help you provide one example of similarity for the regions and one example of difference. Emphasize how to parallel the contrasting information and where to put the comparisons.

Guided Practice: Pass out page 93. Have the class divide into partners. Put the passages on page 92 back on the overhead, and have the partners choose three more differences and two more similarities to fill in the chart. Monitor the partners as they work.

Check for Understanding: As a whole group, refocus the class. Ask for volunteers to share the similarities and differences they discovered. Ask how this information can help them when they compare and contrast things.

Independent Practice: Review the Venn diagram and its purpose. Then, pass out page 94. Ask for a student to explain how to set up the Venn diagram using the two topics. Explain that the students need to find four comparisons and six contrasts. Monitor the students as they complete the Venn diagram independently.

Closure: Review what it means to compare and contrast. Then, ask the students what they discovered when they compared and contrasted the histories of the Central and Southwest states and the River and Lakes states. Ask for some examples of other things in their lives that they can compare and contrast.

Name _____ Date _____

Comparing and Contrasting Natural Resources

The River and Lakes States

Water is an important resource in the Rivers and Lake Region. The Mississippi River has many branches that flow across the states. The five Great Lakes are the biggest lakes in the nation. These water bodies supply water for homes and factories. They are also the main source of transportation for people and goods. They also provide fish as well as places for people to play while on vacation.

The West

The find of gold caused a huge change in the growth of the United States. Once the gold ran out, people began to find other minerals in large amounts. Petroleum, copper, silver, and natural gas are among those most common in the western states. The beauty of the land itself is as much a resource as the minerals. Some states have unusual parts of nature that cannot be found anywhere else in the United States. For example, Yellowstone National Park has geysers, California has redwood trees over 300 feet tall, and Hawaii has unusual trees, flowers and animals. The state governments quickly recognized the land as a resource. Much land is part of parks for safekeeping. The one resource many western states lack is water.

Unit 4: Social Studies

Lesson Plans Using Graphic Organizers 6, SV 2074-5

Name _____ Date _____

Comparing and Contrasting—Venn Diagram

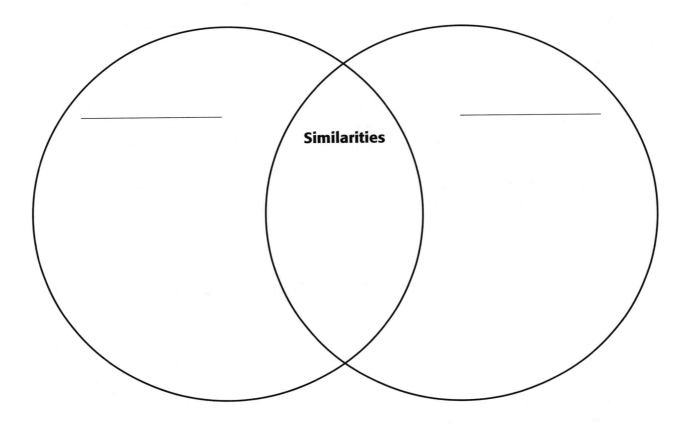

Name _____ Date _____

Comparing and Contrasting Histories

The Central and Southwest States

The Central and Southwest states were slow to settle. There were no trees to build with. Rivers did not flow throughout the land. To help settle the land, the United States government offered settlers 160 acres of land. The people had to live on the land and farm it for five years. The offer was known as the Homestead Act. The government had also given much land to companies to build railroads from the East to the West. The companies wanted to keep the train tracks safe. They invited people from other countries to live in towns they built. Many of these people were farmers. Mining became another way to get settlers into the area.

With the growth of towns, farms, and ranches, the Native Americans were moved off their land. They were forced to live on reservations. Reservations were pieces of land that settlers did not want because the region was dry and not good for farming. The Native Americans attacked wagon trains and farms. The final battle came at Wounded Knee in South Dakota. Many Native American men, women, and children were killed. After this event, most tribes moved to the reservations with little fighting.

The River and Lakes States

For almost a century, France and Great Britain fought over the land. In 1763, Great Britain won the war and got all the land east of the Mississippi River. The land was peaceful for only a few years. The American colonies wanted their freedom. They wanted to make their own laws. They fought with Great Britain in the American Revolution. After that war, the United States owned the land. The new country got more land from the French in a deal called the Louisiana Purchase. The United States now owned land from the east coast to the Rocky Mountains.

Settlers flooded the paths west. They were looking for cheap land, riches, or freedom. Many traveled by rivers or through the Great Lakes on boats. The land was good for farming. Rivers were plentiful and led to the Mississippi River or to the Great Lakes. Goods were easily moved. Cities grew up on the rivers and lakes, too. The first groups of people that moved west were very successful.

Answer Key

p. 8   1. D, 2. C, 3. A, 4. D

p. 10   Main Character: Jake; Feelings will vary along with details.

p. 12   Answers will vary. 1. F: Poison ivy is a common, poisonous plant. O: In the fall, they are a beautiful shade of red.; 2. F: Venus is the brightest object in the sky except for the Sun and Moon. O: It is a lovely name.

p. 13   Answers will vary. 1. F: The king of England sent him to capture pirates in the Red Sea and the Indian Ocean. O: Captain Kidd was a horrible pirate.; 2. F: People learned to raise pigs long ago., O: Many people think that pigs are very dirty.

p. 14   Answers will vary. 1. F: Tropical plants have been found in Antarctica., O: The idea of floating continents is a very interesting one.; 2. F: Some Alaskan bull moose have been measured at $7\frac{1}{2}$ feet at the shoulder., O: The size of these animals is amazing.

p. 16   1. C: Because of an earthquake, 2. E: So they believe the idea is untrue. 3. C: Because the fence would be expensive,

p. 17   1. E: it is grown in a warm climate. 2. C: Because the seeds look like beans to us, 3. E: Bonita was nervous.

p. 18   1. E: they were easy to defend. 2. C: Because there was a period of drought, 3. E: Blanca had her brother pitch to her

p. 20   1. MI: Peter is talented. D: Peter works with his dad to fix things.; He fixed his Aunt Jennifer's car.; Peter fixed his sister's stereo.; take anything apart and fix it. 2. MI: Stephen Foster led an unhappy life. D: He wrote "My Old Kentucky Home."; He died at the age of 38.; He was homeless.; He wrote 200 songs.

p. 21   1. MI: Manuel remembered a special day.; D: fixed his mom breakfast, waxed her car, cleaned his room, baked a birthday cake; 2. MI: Whales are mammals.; D: often mistaken for fish, breathes air, has hair, is warm-blooded, baby whales get milk from their mother

p. 22   1. MI: Roger had many collections.; D: collection of leaves, stamp collections, baseball card collection, coin collection minted in the year he was born; 2. MI: Marcia was cold while she was walking.; D: pulled her scarf tighter, toes felt numb, fingers in her mittens were losing their feeling, wind pushed her along

p. 25   Answers will vary: Who: Bailey and her father, What: went camping, Bailey is scared, Where: the woods, When: at night, morning, Why: to spend time together, Summary: Answers will vary.; Who: Jerry, What: thought there was a burglar in his house, Where: Jerry's house, upstairs, When: during the day, Why: Jerry thought he was home alone, but Grandma was there with her hearing aid turned down; Summary: Answers will vary.

p. 28   Characters: Paul Revere, Setting: Middlesex villages and farms, Plot: Paul Revere was warning the villagers that the British were coming.

p. 30   Characters: Dad and son, Billy, Setting: playground, home, Plot: the boy's dad doesn't want him to play with Billy

p. 32   1. extraordinary, 2. misled, 3. overcome, 4. discontented, 5. foresight, regain

p. 33   Words will vary. 1. M: with, 2. M: not, 3. M: not, 4. M: outside of, beyond, 5. M: former, 6. M: badly, wrong, not, 7. M: not, 8. M: too much

p. 34   Words will vary. 1. M: away, lack of, off, not, 2. M: not, 3. M: before, 4. M: not, the opposite of, 5. M: before, in front of, 6. M: not, 7. M: back, again, 8. M: one

p. 36   1. $1\frac{1}{4}$ ounces, 2. $1\frac{5}{6}$ dozens, 3. 22 flowers, 4. $\frac{4}{5}$ sheet

p. 37   1. 38 smaller meat balls, extra: he bought 2 pounds of beef, 2. 30 slices, extra: she used a $\frac{1}{2}$ cup of nuts and $\frac{3}{4}$ cup of honey in her recipe.

P. 38   1. 15 casts, 2. 8 bandages, 3. 6 days, 4. 26 packages

p. 41   1. 44 in., 2. 132 mm, 3. 88 in., 4. 44 cm, 5. 18.8 m, 6. 75.4 m, 7. 56.5 mm, 8. 12.6 cm, 9. 28.3 in., 10. 94.2 m, 11. 314 sq in., 12. 50.2 sq in., 13. 78.5 sq m, 14. 28.3 sq ft, 15. 7.1 sq in., 16. 32.2 sq cm, 17. 2.5 sq m, 18. 651.1 sq in.

p. 42   1. 9 in., 2. 43.96 in., 3. 78.5 sq in., 4. 3.925 in., 5. 37.68 in., 6. 200.96 sq in., 7. 103.62 sq in., 8. 30 in.

p. 44   1. 304 sq in., 2. 150 sq in.

p. 45   1. length, width, height, 2. Multiply them. 3. cubic inches, 4. $2 \times 2 \times 2$, 5. $3 \times 2 \times 3$, 6. $2 \times 3 \times 2$, 7. 125 cubic in., 8. 6 cubic m, 9. 30 cubic ft

p. 46   Answers will vary according to the boxes you choose to use.

p. 48   1. .240, 2. 21, 3. 9, 4. 45, 5. .360

p. 49   1. 14, 14, 14, 13, 13, 12, 12, 12, 12, 10, 9, 9; 2. 12, 3. 1, 1, 2, 2, 3, 3, 4, 4, 5, 5, 5, 5; 4. 5, 5. Answers will vary.

p. 50   1. 11, 28, 60, 70; 44, 2. 50, 3. 13, 4. 50, 5. Answers will vary.

p. 52   1. Chess: Jacqueline, Reading: Louis, Swimming: Emanuel, Kite flying: Patricia; 2. Coat rack: Eyes, Chef: Ears, Butler: Nose, Fountain: Hands

p. 53 1. Diving: Lynn, Motorcycles: David, Tennis: Laurinda, Kite flying: Angela; 2. Mrs. Ho: Mr. Morozumi, Mrs. Liang: Mr. Ho, Mrs. Morozumi: Mr. Perry, Mrs. Lee: Mr. Liang, Mrs. Perry: Mr. Lee

p. 54 1. Mrs. Washington: Mr. Perrotti, Mrs. Forrest: Mr. Washington, Mrs. Perrotti: Mr. Clark, Mrs. Li: Mr. Forrest, Mrs. Clark: Mr. Li; 2. Ax: D, Rat: B, Flea: A, Jam: E, Gum: C

p. 56 1. (-2, 4), 2. (3, -1), 3. (1, -2), 4. (-4, 2), 5. (-3, -1), 6. (3, 3), 7. A. (3, 4), B. (5, 0), C. (1, -1) D. (-1, 2), E. (-5, -1), F. (4, -4) See grid.

p. 57 See grid.

p. 58 Riddle: It Had To Work Off Its Floppy. See grid.

p. 60 1. Blue, black, red, green, gray 2. Blue, 3. Black, 4. 5/30 or 1/6, 5. 6/30 or 1/5, 6. 22/30 or 11/15, 7. 12/30 or 2/5, 8. 6/30 or 1/5

p. 61 Answers will vary.

p. 62 1. 40, 2. 24, 3. 80, 4. 52, 5. 72, 6. 98, 7. 180, 8. 120

p. 64 2. $63.00, 3. $70.00, 4. $84.00, 5. $78.75, 6. $14.00

p. 65 1. $182.00, 2. $68.00, 3. $90.00/$0.05 = 1,800 kwh

p. 66

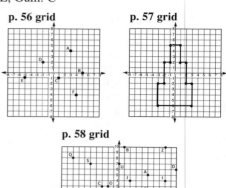

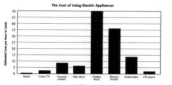

p. 69 Answers will vary.

p. 70 4. Lemon juice: pink, pink, acid; Milk: blue, pink, neutral; Dish soap: blue, blue, base; Sugar water: blue, pink, neutral; Carbonated drink: pink, pink, acid; 5. Lemon juice, carbonated drink, 6. Dish soap, 7. Lemon juice, carbonated drink: An acid turns blue litmus paper pink., 8. Dish soap: A base turns pink litmus paper blue., 9. Milk, sugar water: A neutral substance will not change the color of either blue or pink litmus paper.

p. 72 1. Arctic tundra, 2. Deciduous forests, 3. Deserts, 4. Boreal forests, 5. Grasslands, 6. Tropical rain forests, 7. a large community of plants and animals that is determined by climate and by the kinds of plants found in the area., 8. Answers will vary.

p. 74 1. Brazil, 2. Costa Rica lost much less forest than Brazil., 3. 12,014,000 hectares, 4. Possible responses: Some plants and animals exist only in rain forests; once they are cut down, tropical rain forests take a long time to regrow., 5. Possible answers: learn as much as possible about the rain forests and share this knowledge with others, write letters to public officials, use only products from the rain forest that do not cause permanent damage to the plant and animal life.

p. 76 1. Tall round seeds, yellow seeds, flowers along entire stem, 2. Tall yellow seeds, round seeds, flowers along entire stem, 3. Tall round seeds, yellow seeds, flowers along entire stem

p. 77 Answers will vary according to the survey.

p. 78 Answers will vary.

p. 80 1. prairie grasses, 2. first-order, 3. coyotes, 4. might increase, 5. the bacteria, 6. second-order

p. 81 1. Herring, 2. Shark, 3. The Sun, 4. Plant plankton, 5. Animal plankton would have nothing to eat, so herring would have nothing to eat, and so on. All the organisms in this food chain would eventually die.

p. 82 1. Possible answers: Snakes, toads, spiders, and some birds eat insects. Other birds eat green plants. Hawks and owls eat mice, rabbits, and birds. Rabbits eat green plants. Foxes eat mice and rabbits. Mice eat green plants., 2. The number of rabbits would probably increase, since only hawks and owls would be eating them. But their numbers would probably decrease when competition for food becomes greater., 3. Yes, since the snakes eat the seed-eating birds, they would find food more easily. Their numbers might increase. They might also eat fewer toads and plant-eating insects.

p. 84 1. 10 to 20 inches, 2. Yuma, 3. Flagstaff, 4. Yuma; It receives very little precipitation.

p. 85 1. Population of the North Central Region, 2. A dot, 3. Iowa, 4. 5–49

p. 86 1. Rocky Mountains in Colorado; about 10,000 feet, 2. Mississippi River in Arkansas; sea level, 3. Colorado, Kansas, Oklahoma, Arkansas, 4. about 10,000 feet

p. 88 Answers will vary.

p. 93 Answers will vary. Resources: Same: the regions depend upon their natural resources for livelihood; Difference: the important resource of the River and Lakes states is water; the region has the biggest lakes in the nation; the West's states' important resources are the minerals; the region has little water.

Answers will vary for history: Same: People came from the east to settle out west, land was good for farming, the people were successful; Differences: settlers in the Central and Southwest states were slow to settle the land, the government had to issue land using the Homestead Act, little water, railroads were built to transport goods and connect east to west; settlers in the River and Lakes states flooded the paths west, they wanted cheap land, settlers traveled by rivers and lakes, goods were easily moved along the rivers.